DK THOMAS MARENT
with Tom Jackson

frog

Ghost glass frog
(*Cochranella spinosa*)
with eggs, Colombia

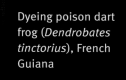

Dyeing poison dart frog (*Dendrobates tinctorius*), French Guiana

File-eared frog (Polypedates otilophus), Borneo

Hyloscirtus lindae, Colombia

Red-backed tree frog
(*Boophis bottae*),
Madagascar

Spendid leaf frog
(*Cruziohyla calcarifer*),
Costa Rica

Glass frog (*Centrolene peristictum*), Colombia

Glass frog (*Centrolenella ilex*), Colombia

Boophis tephraeomystax, Madagascar

Litoria wollastoni, New Guinea

African bullfrog
(*Pyxicephalus
adspersus*),
Madagascar

Flying frog
(*Rhacophorus
pardalis*), Borneo

LONDON, NEW YORK, MELBOURNE,
MUNICH, AND DELHI

PROJECT ART EDITOR Helen McTeer
PROJECT EDITOR Tom Jackson
EDITOR Jamie Ambrose

SENIOR ART EDITOR Ina Stradins
SENIOR EDITOR Angeles Gavira

MANAGING ART EDITOR Phil Ormerod
MANAGING EDITOR Sarah Larter
ART DIRECTOR Bryn Walls
PUBLISHER Jonathan Metcalf

CREATIVE TECHNICAL SUPPORT John Goldsmid
COLOUR REPRODUCTION Adam Brackenbury
PRODUCTION EDITOR Maria Elia
PRODUCTION CONTROLLER Louise Daly

INDEXER Sue Butterworth

First published in Great Britain in 2008
by Dorling Kindersley Limited
80 Strand, London WC2R 0RL

A Penguin Company

Copyright © 2008 Dorling Kindersley Limited
Text copyright © 2008 Dorling Kindersley Limited
All images copyright © 2008 Thomas Marent

2 4 6 8 10 9 7 5 3 1

All rights reserved. No part of this publication
may be reproduced, stored in a retrieval system,
or transmitted in any form or by any means,
electronic, mechanical, photocopying, recording,
or otherwise, without the prior written
permission of the copyright owner.

A CIP catalogue record for this book
is available from the British Library

ISBN: 978-1-4053-3300-9

Colour reproduction by
Media Development Printing Ltd in the UK
Printed and bound in China by Hung Hing Offset
Printing Company Limited

See our complete catalogue at
www.dk.com

contents

a photographer's passion

I find searching for and photographing frogs very special. As a small boy I dammed the creek near my home in Switzerland so that the frogs would have a more hospitable environment. And it meant I could observe them more closely, too. I kept a record of what frogs I saw, carefully illustrating and describing each species. This passion persists today, though I prefer to use a camera to do the work!

My passion for frogs received a big boost on my first visit to a tropical rainforest, when I trekked through northeastern Australia. I became acutely aware of the world's amazing natural diversity. Since then, the rainforest has become my favourite place to photograph wildlife. One of my favourite things is to be in a rainforest when it is raining, listening to the many different calls the frogs are making. It never fails to enthral me.

The variety of colours, shapes, and sounds of frogs is truly spectacular, and a wildlife photographer's dream, literally. On a recent trip to Colombia I found myself dreaming about the beautiful glass frogs I had found. In one particularly vivid part of the dream I was about to marry one! I can remember being captivated by her sheer beauty!

But working in a rainforest does have its drawbacks. As you will see in some of the stories throughout this book, I have had some difficult times in my search for the best frog photographs.

But I am driven to record as much as I can. Today, Earth is facing its largest mass extinction since the disappearance of the dinosaurs. Of the 6,000 or so amphibian species, about 2,000 are in danger of becoming extinct, through habitat loss, climate change, pollution, and collection for food or as pets. The most serious immediate threat is due to a killer fungal disease, which is decimating frog populations across the globe.

Amphibians have been called "the canaries in the coal mine" and are our best indicator of environmental health. As both predator and prey, they help sustain the delicate balance of nature. If we cannot control what is happening to amphibians, what does this say for the future health of our planet?

Thomas Marent

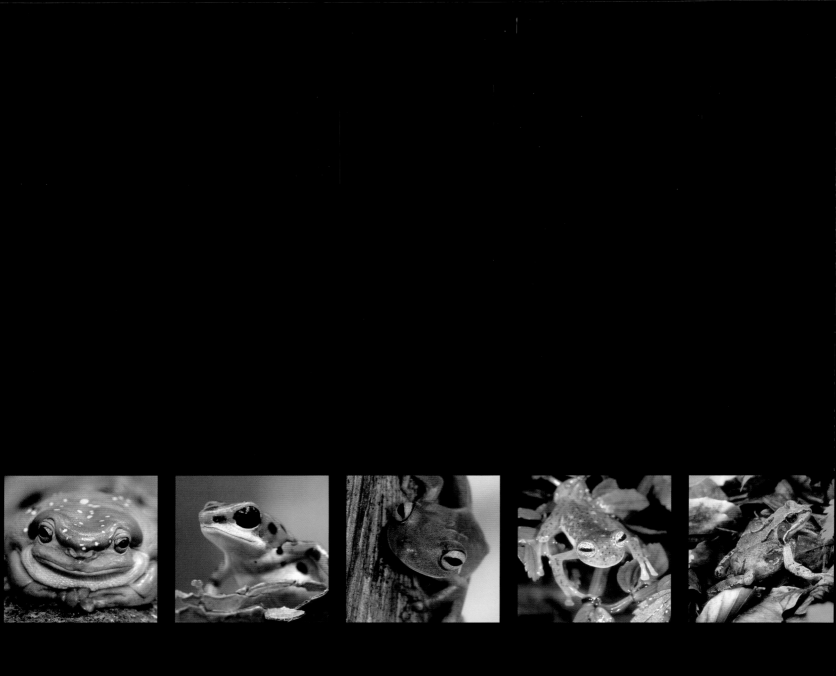

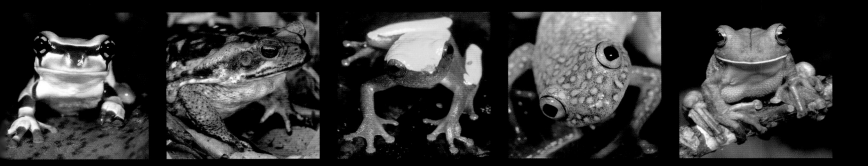

identity

what is a frog?

The answer to this question might seem obvious, but there is a lot more to the world of frogs than warty toads and tadpoles in ponds.

Frogs make up the largest part – about 90 per cent – of the class Amphibia. Amphibians also include newts and salamanders and a few dozen species of rarely seen worm-like burrowers called caecilians.

The big differences between the types are easy enough to spot. The frogs themselves form an order called Anura, meaning "without tail". If ever in doubt about amphibian classification, if it hasn't got a tail, it must be a frog.

Today there are 5,550 recognized species of frog arranged in 30 families. It is sometimes said that amphibians are the most primitive type of land animal; strictly speaking, this really isn't true. It is more likely that frogs and their cousins are a specialized branch of creatures that have evolved to thrive in the warm and damp parts of the world.

About 360 million years ago, the first four-legged animals, or tetrapods, emerged from the shallow seas to walk

△ A spotted-thighed tree frog (*Hyla fasciata*) sits in a cup-shaped toadstool. ▷ A tree frog from Colombia hides out among fallen leaves.

on land. One of these, affectionately known as "Eddie" by scientists, left footprints on the shore of an Irish island. These footprints are now fossilized for all to see. Eddie and his relatives probably had scaly skin covered with hard plates, resembling reptiles more closely than today's soft-skinned amphibians.

The name "amphibian" is derived from a Greek word that means "with a double life". The ancient naturalists had seen that these creatures led a life partly in water and partly on land. The early stages of a frog's life is spent underwater as a tadpole. As it changes into an adult, the frog then begins life in the air. Although the adults might range far from water, they are still tied to it. When it is time to lay eggs, the majority of frogs must find some standing water to provide a nursery for their young.

Frogs are unable to regulate their body temperatures – their bodies are warmed and chilled by the air and water around them. As a result frogs do best in warm, humid places, such as rainforests, where conditions stay more or less the same all year round. Even so some species have adapted to life in colder conditions. Frogs cope with cold winters by becoming torpid – a kind of dormant, hibernation state. Frogs survive dry places by digging into mud and soil when the water runs out.

◁ The long-nosed horn frog (*Megophrys nasuta*) of Malaysia thrives among the damp vegetation of the forest floor.

▷ The American bullfrog (*Rana catesbeiana*) is a highly adaptable species and survives in a range of habitats, but is rarely far from a body of deep water.

▽ The map tree frog (*Hyla geographica)* lives in the humid lowland forests of the Amazon.

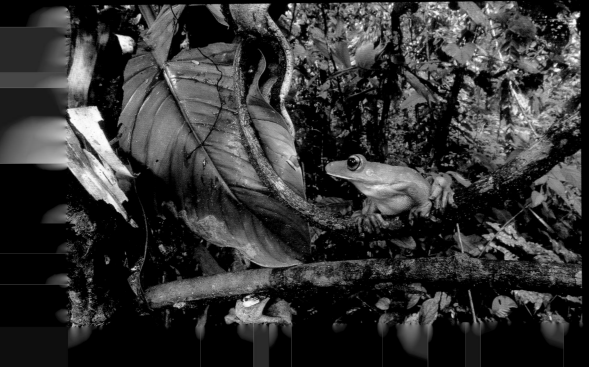

△ The black-spotted rock frog (*Staurois natator*) lives beside forest waterfalls in Borneo.

△ The seep frog (*Occidozyga baluensis*) of Borneo lives on muddy seepage areas, where water flows from forest soil into streams.

△ The ornate burrowing frog (*Limnodynastes ornatus*) takes a dip in Australia after a rainfall.

As well as climbing, the European tree frog (*Hyla arborea*) also uses its long legs to clamber through mud.

▷ A spotted-thighed tree frog (*Hyla fasciata*) crouches on a bracket fungus in the Amazonian rainforest of Peru.

▽ Another tree frog, *Osteocephalus buckleyi*, perches on a toadstool in a Peruvian forest.

A *Mantidactylus grandidieri* rests by a waterfall in Madagascar. Frogs spend most of their time out of sight, but may emerge to bask in warm, damp areas.

" I was exploring the cloud forest of the Manu National Park in Peru with a pair of guides. Hiking upstream, with no real trail, we had to cross over the creek several times to find our way. It was an untouched region, and we were lucky enough to see unusual animals, including the rare quetzal and the spectacled bear. But I was on the lookout for something else: frogs, in particular, glass frogs. In the late afternoon it started to rain heavily and we decided to walk back to the lodge.

Meanwhile, the rain had transformed the creek into a raging torrent. We found that we could no longer cross the river; the risk of being washed away – together with all my equipment – was too high. So we decided to wait, but the water kept on rising. It became very cold and we started to do exercises to keep warm. The thought of having to spend the whole night in the cold was terrifying. But one of the guides was brave enough to risk his life attempting to cross the torrent. He jumped in and swam to the other side, just making it before crashing onto a rock! Then he went back to the lodge for a long rope. When he returned, he threw the rope over to us, so we were able to cross the creek safely, our bags on our heads. "

◁ *Cochranella truebae* glass frogs enjoying the rain of the high, cold forest in the Manu National Park, Peru.

◁ Some tree frogs survive far from the lush jungle. This one is perching on a tree trunk in the region of dry woodland and grassland known as Los Llanos, in Venezuela.

▷ Smaller frogs, such as the strawberry poison dart frog (*Oophaga pumilio*), seen here in Costa Rica, are able to live on the flat surfaces of large leaves.

▽ A *Rhacophorus pardalis* "flying frog" of Borneo climbs through flimsy branches. It does not need to climb to the ground to move between trees, but can make long glides across the forest.

◁ Like other poison dart frogs, the red-banded
Lehmann's poison frog (*Oophaga lehmanni*)
is closely associated with certain plants, such as
bromeliads. The frogs use the valuable source of
water that collects at the base of the leaves.

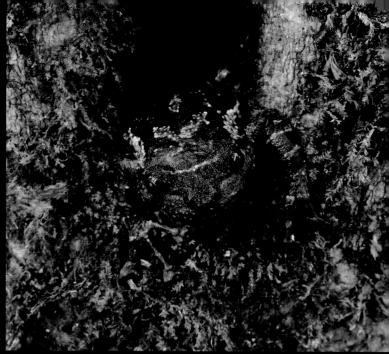

△ The European toad (*Bufo bufo*) spends long periods away from water.

△ This *Platypelis grandis* from Madagascar is keeping moist in a tree hole

△ The European common frog (*Rana temporaria*) is one of the most widespread frog species

TREE FROGS

As their name suggests, frogs belonging to this group spend their lives in the branches. They are the most agile of frogs, characterized by long legs and gripping toe pads used to cling to bark and leaves. However, from a biologist's point of view, tree frogs are not a straightforward bunch. There are three main families of tree frog, but species from other groups have also taken to a similar life in the trees. The largest family of true tree frogs is the Hylidae. This is probably the largest frog family of all, with almost 800 species currently recognized. Most members of the family Hylidae live in the Americas and Australia, but a few also crop up in warm parts of Europe and Asia. Africa's tree frogs belong to the Hyperoliidae. They are also known as reed frogs because they are often found among these plants along river banks. The final family is Rhacophoridae. Its members are found in Africa, too, but are most common in southern Asia. They include the so-called "flying frogs", which glide through the air on outstretched webbed feet.

◁ A map tree frog
(*Hyla geographica*)
in Peru.

△ The white markings of this young Amazon milk frog (*Trachycephalus resinifictrix*) make it easy to see where the species got its name.

△ The white-lipped tree frog (*Litoria infrafrenata*) from Australia is named after the characteristic stripe on its jaw.

△ Leaf frogs of the *Phyllomedusa* genus of South America are also known as walking tree frogs or monkey frogs, due to their remarkable agility.

▷ The stripeless tree frog (*Hyla meridionalis*) is a rare species from southern Europe. It is slighty larger than the common tree frog (*Hyla arborea*), and as its name suggests, lacks the distinctive white stripes on the flanks.

▽ The European tree frog (*Hyla arborea*) is the most common of the two tree frog species living in Europe. It lives further north than the stripeless tree frog. Its distribution extends from the Low Countries to the Ukraine.

The magnificent tree frog (*Litoria splendida*), is a large species from Australia. It was only discovered in 1977. Before that date, the species was thought to be a variant of the more common White's tree frog (*Litoria caerulea*).

△ Variable clown tree frog (*Dendropsophus triangulum*), Peru

◁ Most members of the Hylidae family are
soberly patterned with greens and browns.
However, the clown tree frogs exhibit a range
of bright patterns. This species (*Dendropsophus
leucophyllatus*) from Costa Rica has a skin
pattern similar to that of a giraffe.

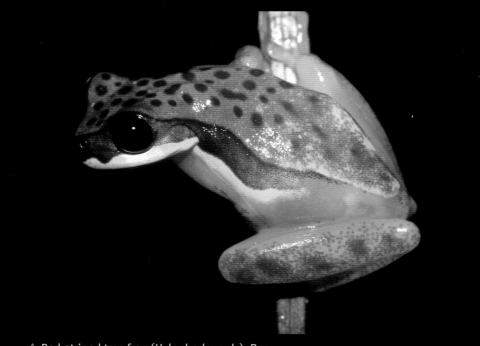

△ Red-striped tree frog (*Hyla rhodopepla*), Peru

leaf frog (*Cruziohyla calcarifer*),

Hourglass tree frogs (*Dendropsophus ebraccatus*) exhibit a range of colour tterns. This specimen has green and brown markings.

△ The hourglass tree frog is named after the curved markings on the back. This specimen is from Costa Rica.

Hypsiboas rufitelus, Costa Rica

This tree frog, *Smilisca phaeota*, from Colombia, ends a lot of time in shallow rivers and marshes.

△ This species of tree frog (*Hypsiboas rosenbergi*), from Colombia and Ecuador, comes to the ground to find mates and lay eggs.

“ A new species of tree frog was discovered in Colombia in 2007; it was given the name *Hyloscirtus tigrinus*. Only two examples had been recorded from the Putumayo region, which is 3000 m above sea level. A scientist friend and I decided to have a look for it in September of that year. We ended up going on my 41st birthday. I would have preferred to celebrate in another way, but the Colombian scientist could only go on that day. He was the only person who knew the exact spot — a small creek in the forest — where we could find the new tree frog. Unfortunately, September is not the breeding season for this species so we would be lucky to find anything. Still, we had to try our luck. It is freezing at that altitude at night, and I couldn't believe that such a large frog species could survive in that environment. I also had other worries: we weren't very far from a dangerous, rebel-controlled region.

After hours searching through the impenetrable vegetation along the creek, we had found nothing. I had given up hope. We couldn't hear the calls of any frogs at all, so we decided to head home. I was thinking, "Why do I do this to myself? Shouldn't I just relax and enjoy my birthday?" I was almost out of the forest when the biologist came over to me. He gave me a big hug and said, "Happy birthday, Thomas." He was holding a member of the rare species. It was beautiful! That was my best birthday present ever. ”

◁ The name *Hyloscirtus tigrinus* has only
recently been confirmed for this species.

◁ *Rhacophorus pardalis* is one
of the flying frogs from the family
Rhacophoridae. This specimen
comes from Borneo. The "flying"
aspect comes from its webbed
feet, which form a gliding surface
when spread out.

▽ *Heterixalus alboguttatus* of
Madagascar belongs to the family
Hyperoliidae, a small group of
tree frogs containing about
200 African species.

GLASS FROGS

At first glance, glass frogs – members of the family Centrolenidae – might look rather unremarkable. Most of these frogs, from the cloud forests of South and Central America, normally look small and green when viewed from above. However, the skin covering their undersides and extremities is largely unpigmented and is so thin in places that it is possible to see the blood vessels running through the body and even the internal organs working away inside. Perhaps ironically, it is this unusual transparency that makes the glass frogs appear unremarkable: background colours show through the frog's minute bodies, helping them stay out of sight among the leaves.

▷ The thin, red blood vessels running through the frogs are clearly visible in this photograph of Fleischmann's glass frog (*Hyalinobatrachium fleischmanni*). The folded white area in the bottom left of the body are the intestines. The heart is also visible in the chest.

IDENTITY

△ *Centrolene callistommum*, a glass frog species living in the wet forest near the northern Pacific coast of South America.

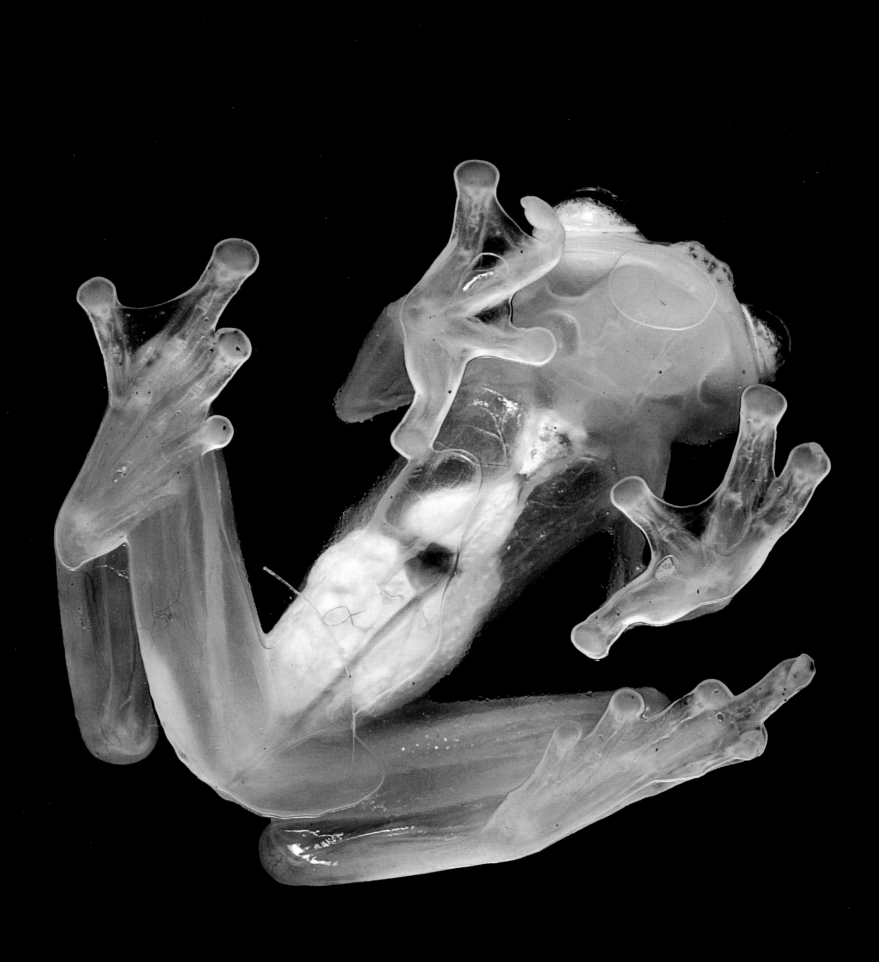

◁ *Cochranella truebae* is a glass frog species endemic to Peru.

▷ Many glass frogs, including Fleischmann's glass frog (*Hyalinobatrachium fleischmanni*), have small spots on their backs.

△ It is hard to tell which part of this *Cochranella truebae* is pigmented green and which areas are coloured by the leaves showing through the transparent skin.

"In the Choco region near Colombia's Pacific coast, I visited a nature reserve in the lowland rainforest. In the afternoon it was raining heavily – perfect weather before a good night of frogging. Unfortunately I became very sick, probably from drinking the water. But I knew that I had to take this great opportunity and go frogging, despite feeling terrible. My guide and I walked along a creek and looked for glass frogs. I was looking on the underside of leaves and found something very rare: a beautiful female glass frog was moistening a clutch of eggs attached to the leaf. The tadpoles inside the eggs were already well developed, and it was almost time for them to hatch. Nearby I also found two beautiful males of the same species (Fleischmann's glass frog). I took lots of pictures.

After a long session editing these images on my camera, I finally had the chance to sleep. I had the weirdest dream ever. I dreamt that I was getting married. I felt very happy and sad at the same time. But why? There were many people there, but no bride. At the end of the dream I got to see my wife-to-be behind a curtain. It was a giant glass frog! I was blown away by the beauty of this frog, which is probably why I felt so happy. But I was also sad because I wasn't single any more."

▷ **Fleischmann's glass frog**
(*Hyalinobatrachium fleischmanni*)

POISON DART FROGS

The Dendrobatidae contains some of the most brightly coloured and appealing frog species of all. The family is also known as the poison dart frogs because of the powerful toxins in the skin of most of its members. The frogs' poisons are traditionally used by the local forest people to coat hunting arrows and blowgun darts. Just touching the frogs is enough for these poisons to aggravate the skin and cause a painful rash. Only a few very toxic species are dangerous to humans, and only then if the toxin gets into the blood via broken skin.

However, not all members of the family produce poisons. The non-poisonous species tend to have green and brown colours that help them blend into the forest background. The poisonous frogs are more brightly coloured.

Unusually for frogs, dendrobatids are diurnal, and their bright colours make them conspicuous in daylight. The colours serve as a warning to predators that the frogs are deadly to eat. In addition, the bright flashes of colour are used by males to attract females.

Photographs of these familiar species often make it hard to visualize the scale of the tiny creatures. Most are less than 3 cm long and could perch on your fingertip – but wear gloves!

◁ The reticulated poison dart frog (*Ranitomeya reticulata*) is found in the rainforests in the Iquitos region of Peru, at the western end of the Amazon Basin.

△ Lehmann's poison frog (*Oophaga lehmanni*) Colombia

◁ The spot-legged poison frog (*Ameerega picta*) is endemic to Bolivia. Poison dart frogs do not make their toxins from scratch. Instead they harvest poisonous alkaloids from the bodies of ants and the other insects they eat.

△ The bamboo poison frog (*Ranitomeya biolat*), Peru

△ Granulated poison dart frogs (*Oophaga granulifera*) live in the lowland forests of Costa Rica and Panama.

◁ The blue form of the dyeing
poison dart frog (*Dendrobates
tinctorius*) is one of the few land
animals to be almost entirely blue.

△ Marbled poison dart frog (*Epipedobates boulengeri*), Colombia

△ Kokoe poison dart frog (*Phyllobates aurotaenia*), Colombia

△ Dyeing poison dart frog (*Dendrobates tinctorius*), French Guyana

△ An alternative colour type of *Dendrobates tinctorius*.

I sometimes try to find animals that are even more toxic that poison dart frogs. A ranger at the Braulio Carillo National Park in Costa Rica told me where to find a very dangerous viper called a terciopelo. Local people are very frightened of this snake, but I got very excited about finding it because I had never taken a picture of the species. The ranger told me to search near a giant fig tree along the trail. He said that the snake had been there for two days. When I finally reached that point, I couldn't see anything. My disappointment did not last long – I discovered a species of anolis. These are green lizards, but when they extend a colourful part on their throat they look stunning. I knew that this normally only happens when they are attracting a female or threatening a rival male. I started to take many pictures of the colourful display, but I couldn't see any other lizards nearby. All my senses were fully concentrated on getting a good shot when something big suddenly jumped on my head. I immediately slapped it away from my head and I was really scared – what if it was the venomous snake? But then I realized that it was only the other anolis lizard that I hadn't noticed before. No wonder: it had been sitting just behind me on the tree all the time. That's why the other lizard was posing so well. Perhaps luckily, I never saw the snake.

▽ The green and black poison dart frog (*Dendrobates auratus*) is one of the more widespread species. It is found in Central America and northern South America.

△ A red and brown form of harlequin poison dart frog (*Oophaga histrionica*).

▷ The harlequin poison dart frog (*Oophaga histrionica*) is named after its bright blotched patterns that resemble the similarly bright costumes of harlequins, or court jesters, from the Middle Ages. The species is not restricted to one set of colours, but also has red and orange forms, or may be yellow and black, like this specimen from Colombia.

△ A yellow, orange, and black form of harlequin poison dart frog.

▷ This harlequin poison dart frog (*Oophaga histrionica*) is standing in a tiny pond that has formed at the base of a bromeliad. Ponds like these are used as nurseries for the frogs' eggs and tadpoles.

△ Yellow-banded poison dart frog (*Dendrobates leucomelas*), Los Llanos, Venezuela

▷ The Golfodulcean poison dart frog (*Phyllobates vittatus*) inhabits the Golfo Dulce region in southwestern Costa Rica. Forest people only use members of the *Phyllobates* genus to make poisons for the darts and arrowheads that give this frog family its common name. The most potent toxins are to be found in the skin on the golden poison dart frog, pictured below. The frog is first impaled on a stick and heated over a fire. The heat drives out the toxin, forming a waxy froth on the skin. This is then wiped very carefully on the tips of arrows. These toxic weapons will paralyse their victims and are ideal for hunting monkeys high in the trees.

△ *Ranitomeya opisthomelas*, Colombia

△ Golden poison dart frog (*Phyllobates terribilis*), Colombia

SPECIES VARIATION: STRAWBERRY POISON DART FROGS

The tiny strawberry poison dart frog, *Oophaga pumilio*, lives in forests and banana plantations across Central America, but it is most common in Costa Rica. Like many types of poison dart frog, this species exhibits more than one pattern of colours; in fact, it has at least 30 distinct colour types, or "morphs". Several of these morphs are associated with specific geographical locations, especially island populations. Some of the colour variations are also due to patterns that develop on the throats of males when they are defending a breeding territory. Whatever their colours, any male and female belonging to this species can breed with one another.

However, biologists have discovered that females of one morph prefer to mate with a male of the same morph. They have also found that some morphs have slightly different mating calls and courtship displays. Perhaps we are seeing evolution in action as the single frog species gradually breaks up into several.

△ The frogs on Isla Bastimentos, an island belonging to Panama, have large black spots on their backs and legs.

△ Bastimentos colour morphs, or "bastis" as they are also known, typically have red, yellow, or white backs.

△ Another Isla Bastimentos morph.

△ Frogs on Isla Colón, also in Panama, often have green skin.

◁ Many of the morphs contain bright-red sections, which is the root of the species' common name.

▽ The red and blue morph – known as the "blue jeans" type – is the most common form, and is a very popular pet among frog enthusiasts.

In common with other poison dart frogs, the strawberry poison dart frog is a minute creature. This specimen is no more than 2 cm from the tip of its snout to the vent (rear opening) – small enough to sit comfortably in this fragile toadstool.

MANTELLAS

This small group of about 15 frog species lives only in Madagascar. They are Africa's equivalent of poison dart frogs. Like their American cousins, these little frogs are active during the day and are brightly coloured to warn predators that their skin contains poisons. Despite these similarities, the two groups of frogs are now known to be only distant relatives. They provide an example of convergent evolution, where unrelated species have developed similar lives and physical characteristis in distant parts of the world. Until recently, the mantellas and their relatives were considered to be members of the Rhacophoridae tree frog family. Today, the mantellas belong to their own family, called the Mantellidae. Most of the bright little mantellas live on or close to the ground, but other members of the family Mantellidae live more conventional tree-frog lifestyles.

▷ The climbing mantella (*Mantella laevigata*) is named after its ability to survive in the branches, which is unusual among mantellas. However, despite the name, this species also lives on the ground. This specimen is living in one of Madagascar's many unusual habitats. A forest that grows in sandy soils not far from the beach-lined coast.

△ The painted mantella (*Mantella madagascariensis*) lives in Madagascar's lowland forests.

△ The green mantella (*Mantella viridis*) lives in the dry forests of Madagascar.

▷ Members of the genus *Boophis* within the family Mantellidae have a more conventional tree frog lifestyle and resemble species from other tree frog families.

▽ The golden mantella (*Mantella aurantiaca*) is a tiny member of the Mantellidae family. It is less than 2.5 cm long and lives on the ground of damp forests.

△ *Boophis boehmei* lives in moist forests.

△ *Boophis bottae* prefers Madagascar's moist forests and forest edges.

△ *Boophis elenae* is one of the few Madagascan species that is found living in artificial habitats such as gardens.

△ *Mantidactylus pulcher* is a member of another genus in the mantella family. It lives in forests and swamps.

△ *Boophis tephraeomystax* lives in forests, swamps and farmland.

△ *Boophis viridis* lives only in lowland forests.

◁ *Boophis viridis* is sometimes
known as the Andasibe tree
frog because it is found in the
wet mountain forests of the
Mantadia Andasibe National Park
in Madagascar. The frog is less
than 3 cm long and it is small
enough to perch on the spiralled
tendrils of a fern.

The Ranidae, or true frog, family is comparable in size to the Hylidae tree frogs, with about 650 species. True frogs are the most widely distributed group of frogs. They live in all continents except Australia and Antarctica. The largest frogs in the world belong to this family, including the bullfrogs and the enormous Goliath frog of Africa (*Conraua goliath*), which can grow to 30 cm long and weighs nearly 4 kg. However, the true frog family is by no means the end of the story. There are currently about 20 more frog families in addition to the dozen or so mentioned in this chapter. Most of them contain just a handful of species and are found in very limited geographical areas.

△ The European common frog (*Rana temporaria*)

◁ A pair of marsh frogs (*Rana ridibunda*) mate in a pool. The marsh frog is one of the parents of the edible frog (*Rana esculenta*); the other parent of this hybrid species is the pool frog (*Rana lessonae*). The hybrid can breed with itself as well as its two parent species.

▷ The long-nosed horn frog (*Megophrys nasuta*) of Malaysia belongs to the family Megophryidae, known as the litter frogs.

▽ More than 400 species of frogs belong to a family called the Microhylidae, or narrow-mouthed frogs. As their name suggests, these species have smaller mouths than other frogs. Most live on or under the ground. Their pointed snouts make it easier for them to dig into soil.

△ A member of the *Amolops* genus of the Ranidae family. Frogs in this genus are known as long-legged frogs. This specimen is from Malaysia.

△ A narrow-mouthed frog from the Manu National Park in Peru, with the typically pointed snout.

△ The red rain frog (*Scaphiophryne gottlebei*) of Madagascar emerges from underground after rain.

▷ There are three species of tomato frog in Madagascar, obviously named after their bright-red colouring. The species shown here is *Dyscophus antongilii*. The tomato frogs are members of the narrow-mouth family, the Microhylidae. The species grow to about 10 cm long, making them larger than most narrow-mouthed frogs.

▷ The Argentine horned frog (*Ceratophrys ornata*) is the most common member of the Leptodactylidae family. It is found across most of Argentina, Uruguay, and Brazil. Despite reaching 14 cm long, the frog is often hard to see because it hides in leaf litter.

△ The Surinam horned frog (*Ceratophrys cornuta*) is one of the largest members of the Leptodactylidae family. The species is confined to South and Central America, the Caribbean, and Florida. Female Surinam horned frogs grow to 20 cm, while the males grow to about two-thirds of this size.

TOADS

"What's the difference between a toad and a frog?" is a question often asked but rarely fully answered. The true toads belong to a family called the Bufonidae. Many familiar toads, such as the American toad and European common toad, belong to a genus, or subgroup, within this family, called *Bufo*. Any animal with *Bufo* in its name is definitely a toad.

But unfortunately, the answer is not that simple. Some species are known as toads but do not belong to the Bufonidae. These include the spadefoot toads (family Pelobatidae). To add to the confusion, even some members of the Bufonidae are known as frogs.

So in the end we must fall back on a more general definition. Toads tend to spend more of their time out of water and move with short hops, although they can make longer leaps if needed. They have broad, rounded snouts compared to the pointed faces of the more aquatic frogs. Toads also tend to have warty skin in contrast to the smooth skin of frogs. But as ever, there are many and varied exceptions to these rules.

◁ The *Bufo* genus has more than 250 members. This one, *Bufo margaritifer*, lives on the floors of lowland tropical forests in northern South America.

△ Native to South and Central America, the marine toad has also been introduced to Australia, where it is known as the cane toad and is a pest. The species has been named *Bufo marinus*, *Chaunus marinus*, and, more recently, *Rhinella marina*.

△ Pebas stubfoot toad (*Atelopus spumarius*), French Guiana

△ Elegant stubfoot toad (*Atelopus elegans*), Colombia

△ Cayenne stubfoot toad (*Atelopus flavescens*), French Guiana

△ Panamanian golden frog (*Atelopus zeteki*), Panama

△ The Condoto stubfoot toad (*Atelopus spurrelli*), Colombia

△ Condoto stubfoot toads live in the lowlands of Colombia.

◁ Members of *Atelopus*, a genus in the Bufonidae toad family, are known as the harlequin toads – or sometimes frogs. They look nothing like their large, warty cousins, but are instead small, brightly coloured species. Their distribution extends from Costa Rica to Bolivia and French Guiana. Most live in forests growing at high altitude. A few species have poisonous skins.

▽ The natterjack toad (*Epidalea calamita*) is a small European species. It can be distinquished from the common toad by a yellow line that runs down its back.

△ The sharp-nosed toad (*Bufo dapsilis*) lives among the fallen leaves.

◁ Despite its name, the European common toad (*Bufo bufo*) lives in three continents. Its range extends west across the whole of Europe and carries on all the way to western Siberia. The species also lives in the mountains of North Africa. Females of this species can grow to 18 cm, making it by far the largest toad species in the region.

▷ The yellow-bellied toad (*Bombina variegata*) lives in central and southern Europe (except Spain). It is minute compared to other toads in the area, growing to between 3.5 and 5 cm long. It belongs to the family Bombinatoridae.

△ The midwife toad (*Alytes obstetricans*) belongs to a separate family: the Alytidae. Despite its name, it is the male that carries the eggs until they hatch. This species lives in mainland Europe and northwestern Africa.

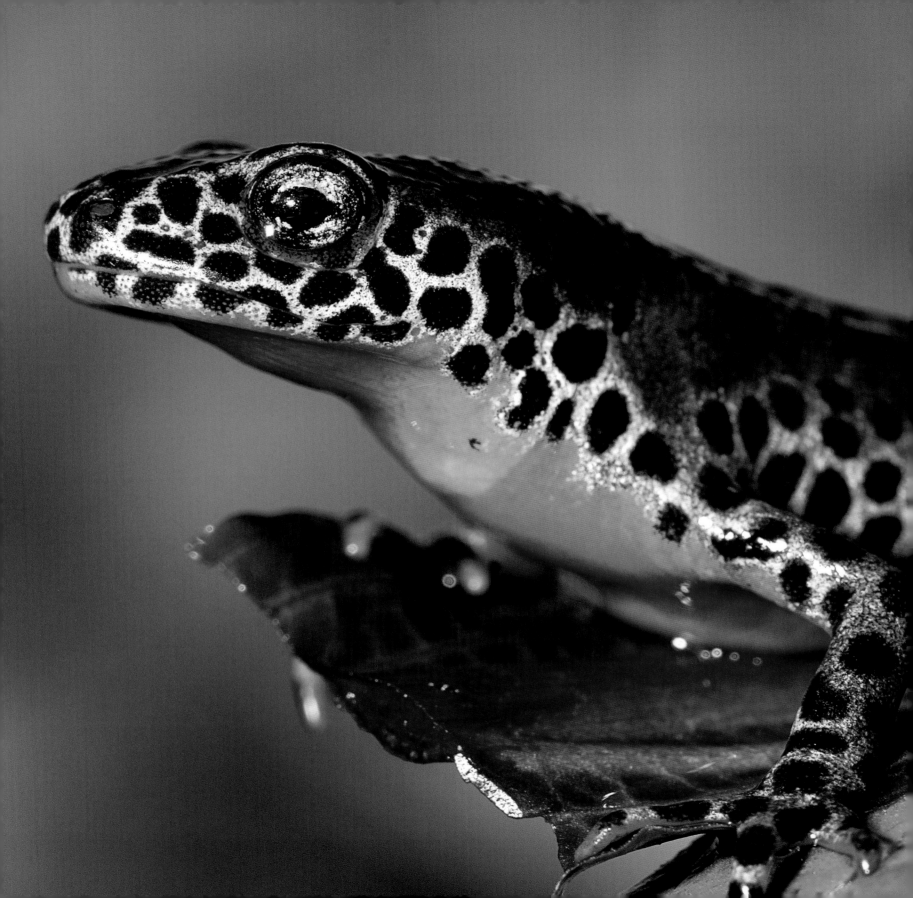

NEWTS AND SALAMANDERS

About one in ten amphibians belongs to the order Caudata, a name meaning "the tailed ones". Most members of the Caudata are newts and salamanders. The difference between a newt and salamander is as unclear as the frog/toad issue. In general, newts live in or close to water, while salamanders range much further afield across land. Of all the amphibians, it is perhaps the salamanders that have loosened their ties with water the most. Some have evolved a completely terrestrial life cycle. However, it should be noted that these salamanders are not the ancestors of lizards and other reptiles, despite having similar body shapes.

The Caudata also includes several other types of unusual creatures with strange names, many of which are entirely aquatic. For example, the olm is a blind, pink newt that lives in lightless, flooded caves. Mudpuppies are named after the yelps they make when handled. The largest living amphibian, the Japanese salamander, also belongs to the order Caudata. It is a rarely seen monster that grows to 1.5 metres long.

◁ A male alpine newt (*Mesotriton alpestris*). This species lives in the streams and lakes of northern and eastern Europe, with a few pockets in highland areas further south. They hibernate in winter.

△ A male great crested newt (*Triturus cristatus*). This widespread species lives in most of Europe, except Ireland and northern Scandinavia. Males only develop the eponymous crest during the breeding season.

◁ The fire salamander (*Salamandra salamandra*) lives in central and southern Europe. The word *salamander*, meaning "fire-lizard" in Greek, comes from a mythical creature associated with fire that was perhaps inspired by this species.

△ Most fire salamanders are yellow and black, but this juvenile belongs to a rare orange variant. The coloured markings can be in the form of blotches and or bands.

△ The palmate newt (*Lissotriton helveticus*) is one of three Caudata species to live in Britain. The species also lives across western Europe, from northern Spain to Denmark.

body form

frog features

Despite the huge number of frog species and their great wealth of sizes and survival strategies, frogs all share a very similar body structure.

The basic frog body is comprised of a large, wide head, a short spine, and four legs. Famously, a frog's back legs are much longer than those at the front. These are the engines behind the hops and leaps that frogs use to move around a range of land habitats, and as paddles when they are swimming. The back legs are anchored to a similarly robust pelvic girdle. In slender frogs, the bones of this large girdle are often visible as a hump on the lower back.

As frogs reach adulthood and transform from swimming animals into land-based ones, they lose their paddle-shaped tails – structures which could be a potential hindrance to jumping animals.

One of the great successes of the first land vertebrates was to evolve a flexible neck. This was a move away from the sleek, streamlined body of fish and allowed the first amphibians to move their heads from side to side. Salamanders have retained this feature. However,

△ Frogs rely on their eyes more than most animals. The eyes even help with swallowing.
▷ A lemur leaf frog (*Phyllomedusa lemur*) shows off the large eyes and long legs that have made the frog body form such a successful one.

frogs have sacrificed a flexible neck in return for a sturdy one that can hold a large head. Frogs evolved as specialist insect eaters, and their large heads give them wide mouths: the perfect tools for catching bug prey.

EYES

Sight is the dominant sense for frogs. The vast majority rely on it to find their food. Like other hunters, frogs have eyes located toward the front of the head, enabling them to focus on the area before them when searching for prey. However, being unable to turn its head means that a frog cannot scan its surroundings for approaching danger; it needs to shift its entire body to look straight at an object. Instead, the frog relies on the orientation and size of its eyes to give it a wide field of view – they point slightly outward at an angle rather than straight ahead. Although this orientation reduces the frog's ability to see things in pin-sharp detail, it does allow it to see a lot of its environment all at once. The eyes are especially sensitive to movement; frogs find it difficult to see motionless prey.

Most frogs are nocturnal, and they need large eyes that can collect enough light to see in the dark. Their wide heads are robust enough to carry huge eyes: much of each side of the skull is given over to a hole, or orbit, where the eye sits and connects to the brain.

The retinas of some species have a "mirror layer", called a tapetum lucidum, behind it. This reflects any light missed the first time onto the retina. It is this reflected light that makes the eyes shine when frogs are caught in torchlight.

◁ The frog eye focuses by using a lens, just as mammalian eyes do. However, instead of changing shape to focus light, as in human eyes, the frog's stiff lens is moved back and forth in the eye.

▷ Most frogs, such as this walking tree frog (*Phyllomedusa vaillanti*) are nocturnal. As a result, they have few colour-sensitive cone cells in their retinas. Instead they rely on rod cells, which are more sensitive in low light levels. A frog's rod cells are most sensitive to the mid-range of light wavelengths: the greens and yellows. In general, frogs cannot really see red light.

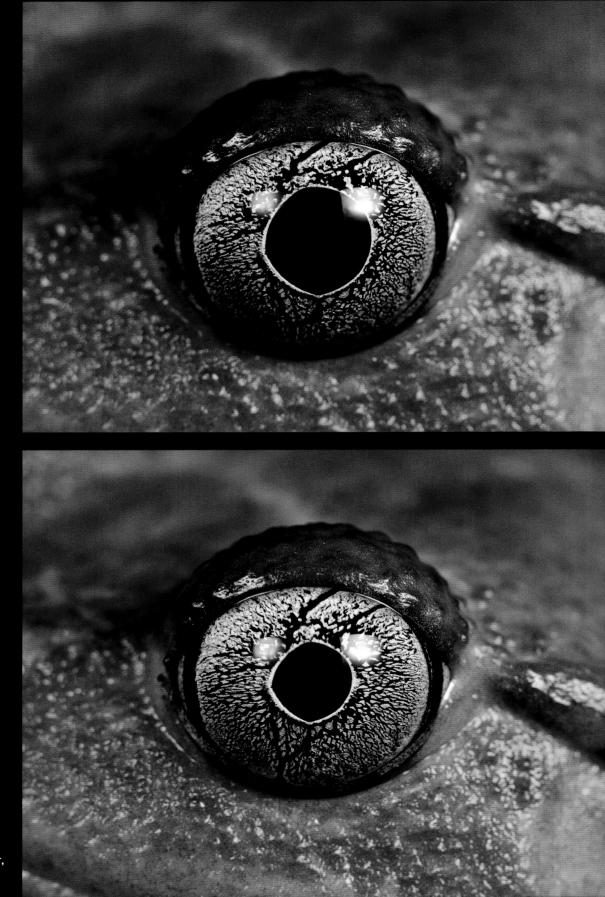

▷ Ground-dwelling frogs, such as bullfrogs or toads, tend to have round pupils. Just as in human eyes, the iris contracts and expands to reduce the amount of light entering the sensitive interior, as in this eye of a tomato frog (*Dyscophus antongilli*).

◁ Tree frogs have diamond-shaped irises. This shape is best for low light levels, because it can open very wide in the dark – wider than a round iris – and then close to a slit in bright conditions. The red-eyed leaf frog (*Agalychnis callidryas*) has vertical pupils, which make its eyes most sensitive to horizontal motion, such as an insect walking along a branch.

▽ This tree frog from the Los Llanos savanna region of Venezuela has horizontal pupils. These make its eyes sensitive to vertical motion, such as insects walking up a tree trunk.

◁ This image of a *Hypsiboas crepitans* tree frog shows the nicticating membrane, or "third eyelid", opening. The clear membrane is used as an extra protective layer; swimming frogs use theirs as a pair of goggles, although the membrane reduces visual acuity considerably.

△ The nicticating membrane of a *Boophis tephraeomystax* of Madagascar opens as the frog wakes up.

Most frogs, such as the American bullfrog (*Rana catesbeiana*), have large, bulging eyes on the tops of their heads. When a frog's body is hidden in water, its eyes poke through the surface so it can keep a lookout for prey.

△ Green-eyed frog (*Litoria genimaculata*),
Palmerston National Park, Australia

△ *Centrolene callistommum* glass frog

△ *Osteocephalus taurinus,* Colombia

△ Fleischmann's glass frog (*Hyalinobatrachium fleischmanni*), Colombia

△ The black-spotted rock frog (*Staurois natator*), Borneo

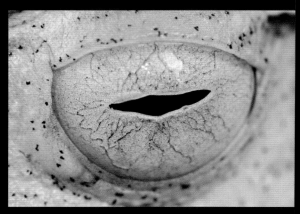

△ The file-eared tree frog *(Polypedates otilophus),* Born

△ A tree frog, *Hyla rubracyla*, from Colombia

△ Strawberry poison dart frog (*Oophaga pumilio*)

△ A tree frog from the Morrocoy National Park, Venezuela

△ A pair of natterjack toads (*Epidalea calamita*)

△ The yellow-bellied toad (*Bombina variegata*) has heart-shaped pupils. No one is quite sure of the purpose of this shape. Similar keyhole-shaped pupils are seen in other animals, which use them to focus on small, fast-moving prey. It has been suggested that the vague stripes on the toad's upper lip form a series of "guidelines". The toad uses these lines to pinpoint flying insects that move past its face.

The *Hypsiboas crepitans* tree frog from Venezuela's Los Llanos region – a dry area whose name translates as "the plains".

At first glance it might appear that frogs are earless creatures, but their ears are in fact quite easy to spot if you take a closer look. Frogs do not have a pinna, or outer ear, like mammals, but the rest of the ear is similar to our own. Behind the eye you can normally see a round, flat structure. This is the eardrum. Sound waves – vibrations in the air – beat against this thin membrane of skin, making it wobble. Behind the eardrum is a small cavity, which contains the middle ear. This feature is an important difference between land vertebrates and their fish ancestors. The middle ear contains a series of tiny bones that transmit the vibrations of the eardrum to the inner ear. (The current thinking is that these middle-ear bones are derived from fish jawbones. The ear cavity itself might have evolved from a fish's breathing tube, or spiracle.) The inner ear contains a fluid-filled bone, where the physical vibrations are converted into an electrical signal that can be interpreted by the brain.

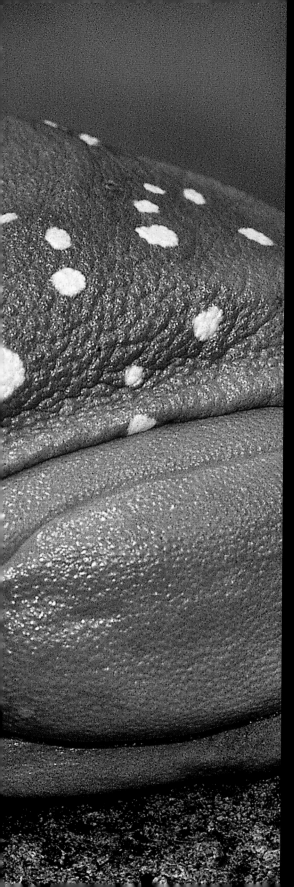

◁ Despite belonging to a different family of tree frogs, the eardrum of the magnificent tree frog (*Litoria splendida*) looks very similar to that of its distant cousin below. The ears of all amphibians are structured in the same way.

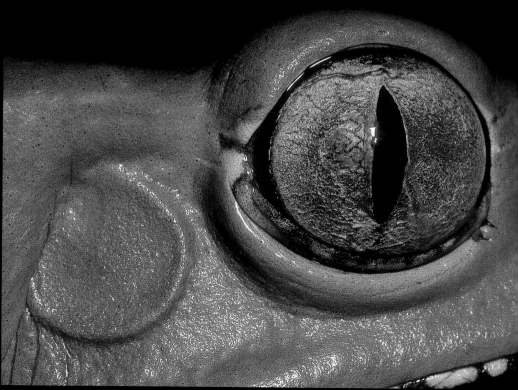

△ The eardrum is clearly visible on the head of this walking

▷ The eardrum of *Eleutherodactylus w-nigrum* of Colombia is hidden under the shoulder ridge. In some species, especially toads, the eardrums are not visible at all.

△ The eardrum of a long-legged frog of the genus *Amolops* from Malaysia is coloured o make it a part of the species' overall pattern.

△ The main purpose of a frog's ear is to listen for the calls made by other frogs, such as this dainty green

frogs have tiny nostrils on their snouts. The primary function of these is breathing, rather than smelling. Frogs do have a strong sense of smell. They use it primarily to find mates, by heading towards the odours released by members of the opposite sex.

Most of the animal's odour-sensitive cells are located on the roof of its mouth rather than in the nasal cavity; thus, when a frog needs to "sniff" the air, it opens and closes its mouth. The structure in the mouth that it uses for this task is called the Jacobson's organ.

Frogs evolved from fish, but fish that were rather different to the ones we are familiar with today. These ancient fish lived in shallow, stagnant water. They breathed water through gills but also took breaths of air with primitive lungs when needed. Other land vertebrates (mammals, birds, and reptiles) that evolved from the same ancestor have done away with gills completely and now breathe solely with lungs. However, in the early stages of their life cycle, frogs still employ gills, while adults are able to take in oxygen through areas of thin skin as well as through the nostrils.

▷ As well as breathing through their skin, frogs can also smell with it. The surface of the eyes – such as those of this *Eleutherodactylus w-nigrum* – are especially sensitive to scent chemicals in the air.

△ Despite having such large mouths, frogs such as this White's tree frog (*Litoria caerulea*) breathe through the nostrils with their mouths closed. Oxygen passes into the blood via the lungs, but frogs can also collect oxygen through the moist lining of their throats. The lining of the frog's large throat

FEET AND LEGS

The frog body plan has proved remarkably successful. Hopping is an effective way of getting around almost anywhere, from a mud-flat to the topmost branches of trees. It is especially good for moving back and forth between water and land, a place frogs dominate. As a result, frogs have needed to vary their body plan only slightly to accommodate the requirements of different habitats.

Features that show some variation are the limbs. In general terms, species that spend more time on land, such as toads, have shorter back legs than a typical frog. Front and back legs of similar lengths are more suited to the problems posed by clambering over uneven ground. However, this ability comes at the expense of some leaping capabilities. The best leapers, such as tree frogs, have very long hind legs. They fold into spring-loaded levers that can catapult the animal up and forward to escape predators, catch prey, or jump between branches.

A frog's digits also vary according to it lifestyle. Climbing species need fingers and toes that will grip well. They need to be able to wrap around twigs and tend to be more flexible than the digits of aquatic frogs, which are stiffened into paddles used in swimming.

▷ As this photograph of a dainty green tree frog (*Litoria gracilenta*) shows, a frog's back leg has four joints. The section third down from the hip is made of elongated tarsus bones; in humans these bones are all contained within the ankle. The fourth and final section contains the digit, or toe, bones.

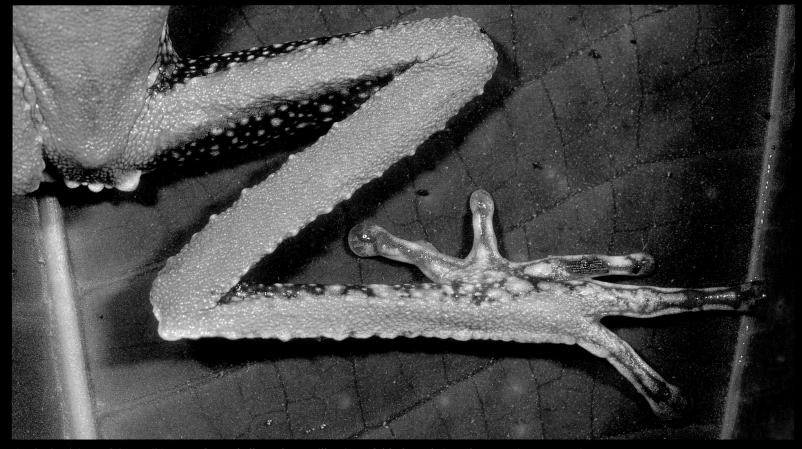

△ The back legs of this walking tree frog, *Phyllomedusa vaillanti*, are folded neatly into three sections. The frog can throw itself forward by straightening all of the leg joints rapidly at the same time.

A red-eyed leaf frog (*Agalychnis callidryas*) uses its long legs and flexible fingers and toes to walk along a narrow branch in the Cahuita National Park, Costa Rica.

Long, flexible legs are seen in most members of the two main tree frog families, the Hylidae and Rhacophoridae. However, the pelvic bones of the Asian tree frogs (Rhacophoridae) show that they are more closely related to the true frogs (Ranidae). Both sets of tree frogs have evolved long legs independently in response to the challenges of living in trees.

△ The dainty green tree frog (*Litoria gracilenta*) is an Australian member of the family Hylidae.

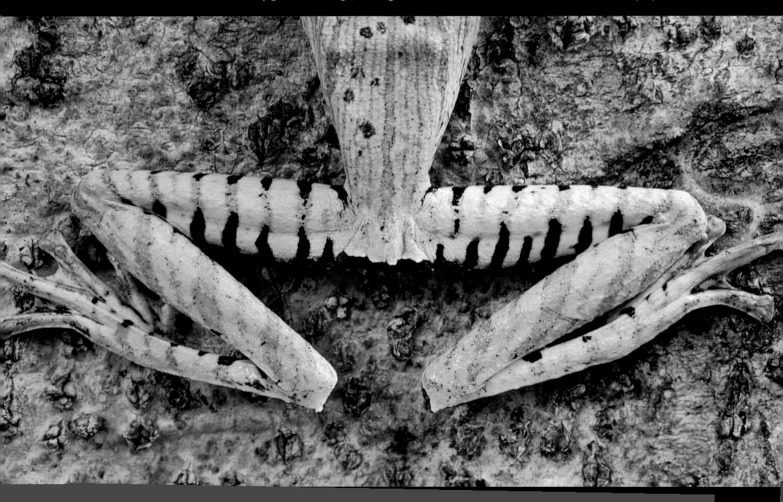

Many species of frogs and toads have webbed hind feet. In most cases, the webbing is used to turn the back feet into paddles for swimming. However, webbing is also used for gliding (as in the case of flying frogs) and digging. The best example of the digging function is seen in the spadefoot toads of the family Pelobatidae. These medium-sized frogs are found across the northern hemisphere in areas with loose soil, such as the North American Great Plains. Their webbed back feet also have a sharp-edged "spade" on the inner toe, which the spadefoots use to bury themselves in order to escape the heat of the day.

△ The long toes of these European common frogs (*Rana temporaria*) are heavily webbed for swimming.

s *pardalis* is a
obed feet are n

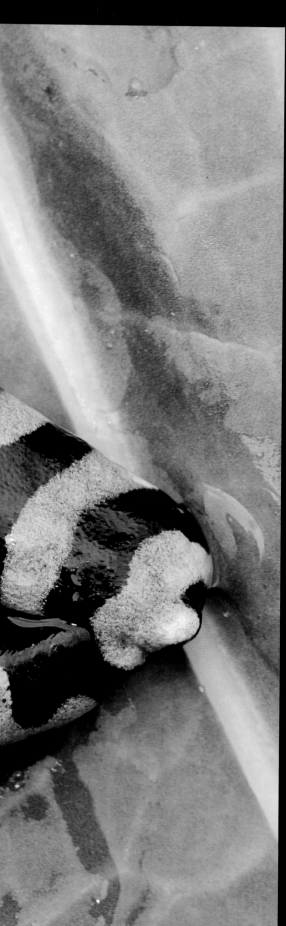

◁ Most frogs have five toes.
Although it may be hard to see
in some specimens, each toe
contains the same number of
bones and joints as a human's.

△ The majority of frogs have four fingers, seen here on the forefoot of a *Hyloscirtus lindae* tree frog.

△ The dainty tree frog (*Litoria gracilenta*) is light enough to cling to a leaf.

△ Toe pads are handy for walking over fallen leaves.

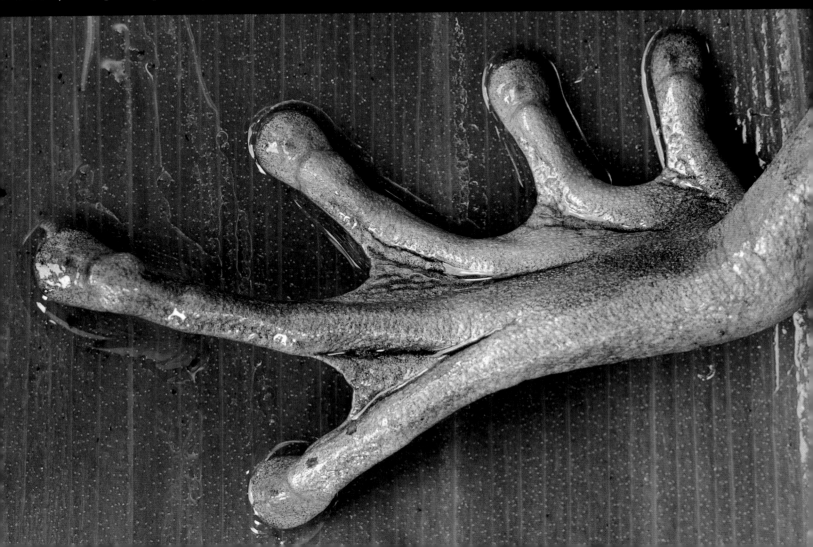

△ Tree frogs of all types have pads on their toes.

△ A clown tree frog (*Dendropsophus triangulum*), Peru

△ The black-spotted rock frog (*Staurois natator*) uses its pads to cling to wet rocks.

The toe pads of tree frogs are often described as suckers. In fact, the use of suction is rare among land animals. Instead, the pads have tiny ridges on them that grip smooth surfaces – just like the tread of a tyre or the sole of some shoes.

▷ It is not unusual for ground-living frogs to have bulbous tips to their fingers as well. However, most of them, including Madagascar's tomato frog (*Dyscophus antongilii*), have long, thin fingers and toes.

△ This rain frog from Peru belongs to the genus *Eleutherodactylus*. The genus name means "free toed": no member has any webbing at all.

△ Like other members of the Dendrobatidae, strawberry poison dart frogs spend most of the time on the ground, and so have thin digits.

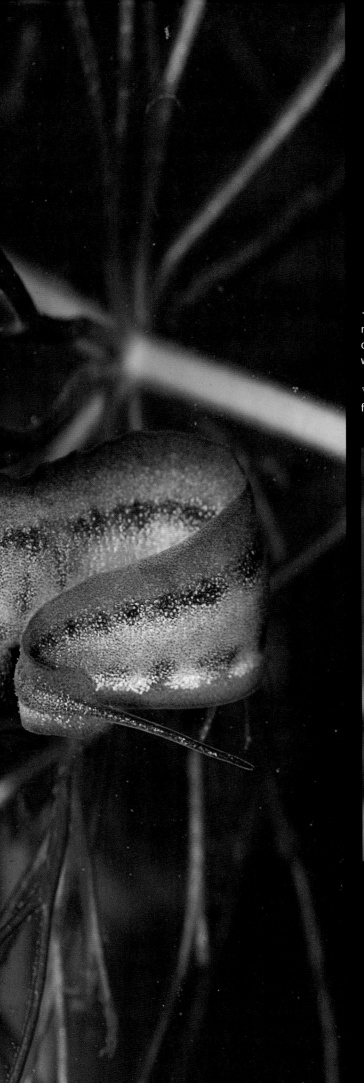

◁ The four legs of this palmate newt (*Lissotriton helveticus*) are of similar length because newts walk, rather than hop, on land.

▽ Like most frogs, newts have four fingers and five toes.

SKIN

Human skin is often described as a barrier between our body and the environment. However, to a frog, the skin is its interface with its surroundings: both water and gases can pass through it. Frogs do not need to drink; they can absorb water through their "seat pouch", an area of thin skin on the belly. But what goes in can come out again. Most frogs cannot survive without a ready supply of water, be it moisture in the air of a humid jungle or running water from a stream. Without it they would dry out and die. Glands in the skin produce mucus that provides a waterproof barrier and slows water leaving the body.

△ The green-eyed frog (*Litoria genimaculata*), an Australian tree frog, has rough skin compared to many of its relatives.

△ The strawberry poison dart frog (*Oophaga pumilio*) secretes toxic mucus onto its skin.

△ Unusually for a member of the *Atelopus* genus, this species, *A. erythropus*, from Peru, has rough skin.

△ The map tree frog (*Hyla geographica*) is named after the blotches that appear on its scaly skin, which are said to resemble land masses on a map.

△ This *Eleutherodactylus* species has a very striking skin texture. The genus *Eleutherodactylus* belongs to the

△ European tree frogs (*Hyla arborea*) have moist, smooth skin.

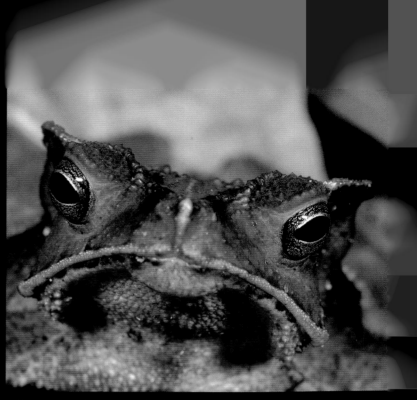

△ This crested forest toad (*Bufo margaritifer*) has distinctive ridges.

◁ Toads are known for their warty skin, which helps them to blend in among the leaves and soil of their habitat. The large lumps, or parotid glands visible here on the head of the common toad (*Bufo bufo*), contain poisonous liquids that burst out when the animal is handled roughly.

▽ The Argentine horned frog (*Ceratophrys ornata*) has very distinctive rough markings. The greens, oranges, and yellows make it stand out when seen by itself, but they work as ideal camouflage in the wild.

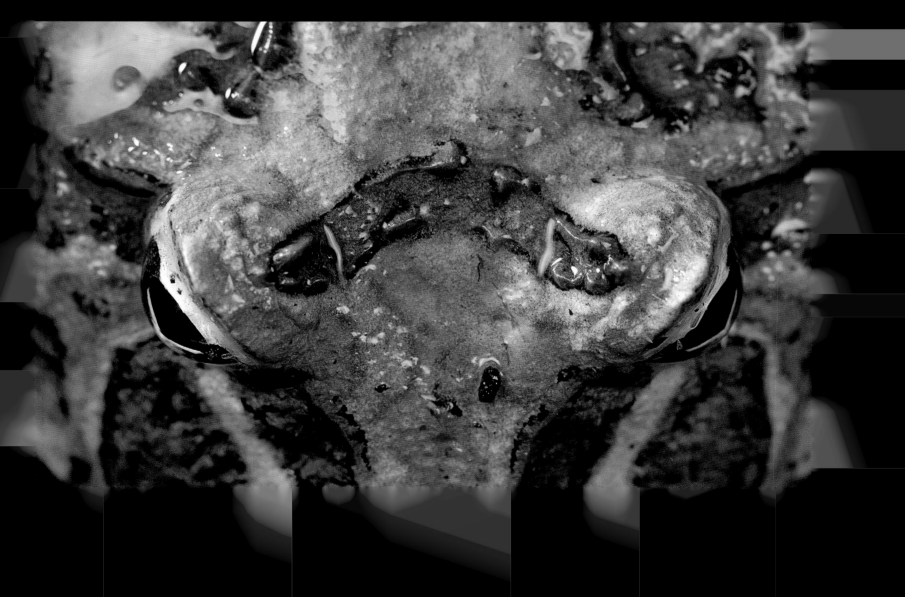

◁ The long-nosed horn frog (*Megophrys nasuta*) of Malaysia is named after its pointed snout. The frog also has two "horns" above its eyes. The function of the horns is to resemble the tips of leaves so that the frog can hide among the leaf litter. The deception is aided by ridges, which look like the edges of leaves, that run along its back.

△ The Argus reed frog (*Hyperolius argus*) of Kenya is a colourful member of the Hyperoliidae, an African tree frog family.

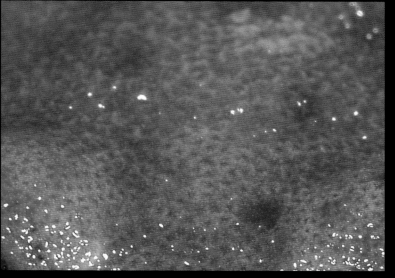

△ Spotted tree frog (*Hyla punctata*)

△ Argentine horned frog (*Ceratophrys ornata*)

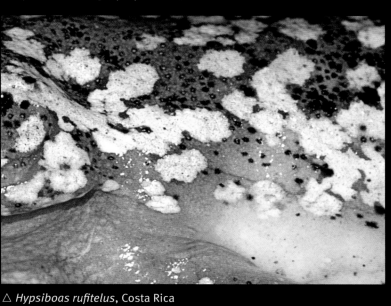

△ *Hypsiboas rufitelus*, Costa Rica

△ Asian tree frog (*Rhacophorus* species)

△ Surinam horned frog (*Ceratophrys cornuta*), Surinam

△ *Dendropsophus leucophyllatus*, Costa Rica

▷ Frogs have only small lungs and most also take oxygen in through the skin. For smaller frogs, this process – known as cutaneous respiration – is actually the fastest route for oxygen to travel to the body tissues. Gas exchange, in which oxygen passes into the blood, while waste carbon dioxide leaves the body, can take place only across damp surfaces. Frogs, such as *Gastrotheca ruiza,* have to moisturize their skin regularly with mucus glands to keep the gases flowing. This species is one of the so-called "marsupial frogs". The females store eggs in a back pouch, where they develop into froglets.

△ The skin pattern of several frogs has earned them the name *harlequin*. Seen here on the left is the harlequin poison dart frog (*Oophaga histrionica*) of northern Colombia. On the right is *Atelopus zeteki*, a harlequin frog from a few miles further north in Panama.

survival

a frog's life

As frogs leap through life in a continuous search for food and mates, they must also be on constant alert for a wide range of predators.

Life is short for a frog. The majority of them die as tadpoles, snapped up by fish, insects, and even other frogs. If they make it through their perilous youth, the average species is lucky to see out its third year. However, larger frogs enjoy more of a future; some, including the common toad and horned frogs, survive for a decade or more. Some of the longest-lived species, the tailed frogs of the Pacific northwest (family Ascaphidae), live for 20 years.

A frog's life is a simple one, with a short list of requirements: water, food, warmth. Frogs don't need to co-operate with other frogs in order to achieve these, and as a result are mostly solitary creatures, with little social life to speak of outside the breeding season. They may congregate by chance around a good feeding site, but actively avoid each other unless it is time to breed.

Many frogs, notably poison dart frogs, will vigorously defend a small feeding

△ The key to survival for many frogs is staying out of sight. This European common frog (*Rana temporaria*) is keeping a low profile among the pebbles of a stream bed. ▷ The dyeing poison dart frog's (*Dendrobates tinctorius*) bold survival strategy is to be clearly visible – warning others to stay away.

and breeding territory. Most fights involve a bit of pushing and shoving and a lot of loud calling. The male gladiator tree frog even has some weaponry at its disposal: sharp spines on each back foot,

FEEDING

All adult frogs are carnivores. Most are insect eaters, although aquatic species consume a wider range of foods, including fish and tadpoles. Unlike those of mammals, a frog's tongue is attached to the front of its mouth, just behind the lower jawbone. This position makes it easier for the tongue to unfurl quickly and strike prey.

While able to taste with its tongue, a frog relies mainly on the Jacobson's organ in the roof of its mouth to detect the presence of chemicals in its food. In this way, different species are able to select foods that are most beneficial to them.

Poison dart frogs are a case in point. Studies have shown that if bred in captivity and fed diets of non-toxic insects, they quickly lose their protective skin poisons. However, when given a choice, they will actively choose food items containing toxins – including their own shed skins – in order to "top up" the beneficial poisons in their bodies.

◁ Horned frogs, such as this species, *Ceratophrys cornuta*, from Peru, are renowned as frog-eating frogs. Their giant mouths have earned them the name "Pac-Man frogs", after the famous 1980s video game.

△ A palmate newt (*Lissotriton helveticus*) preys on the tadpole of a common frog (*Rana temporaria*).

△ At 20 cm long, American bullfrogs are large enough to tackle a range of prey, from snakes and crayfish to younger members of their own species.

◁ Unsurprisingly, "narrow-mouthed" frogs have small mouths. As a result they can prey only on small insects. Many, including the Bolivian bleating frog (*Hamptophryne boliviana*), named after its distinctive call, feed almost exclusively on ants.

▷ Sometimes catching prey is easy: a mosquito has landed on the head of this dainty tree frog (*Litoria gracilenta*).

△ This rain frog (genus *Eleutherodactylus*) is waiting beside a sundew plant. Sundews are carnivorous plants, which trap insects in their sticky tentacles. The frog might be waiting for an easy meal to arrive.

A friend of mine in Switzerland gave me a great tip on how to get some edible frogs to pose for this photograph. We took a stick with a string, like a fishing rod, and put a colourful flower on the end of the string. Then we let the flower bounce near the water's surface. All the frogs in the area swam towards the "dancing flower" and seemed to be hypnotized by it. They probably thought it was a potential meal, like a colourful dragonfly or damselfly. Soon they were all sitting close together and I could take a few shots.

SURVIVAL

▷ Several edible frogs (*Rana esculenta*) pose on a log while under the influence of Thomas's "dancing flower".

◁ A European common frog (*Rana temporaria*) collects prey with its long tongue. A frog's tongue is a wide pad smeared with gooey mucus, which sticks to small prey such as insects.

▷ A green frog (*Lithobates clamitans*), a large species from eastern North America, captures a dragonfly meal.

▽ An edible frog (*Rana esculenta*) slowly swallows an earthworm. The frog will use its eyes to help swallow such a large meal: by retracting them into its head, they push down on the roof of the mouth. This extra pressure helps to force food down the throat.

Most frogs ambush their prey. This Argentine horned frog (*Ceratophrys ornata*) is hiding out in leaf litter, waiting for more or less anything that will fit in its huge mouth. The frog uses its hind feet as a lure, placing them on its back and wiggling them enticingly.

METHODS OF MOVEMENT

Hopping can be a very efficient way of getting around. The average frog can propel itself forward more than ten times its body length in a single bound. The forces involved in such a feat take their toll; however, a frog's body is specially strengthened to withstand the repeated stresses of each jump.

The bones of the lower leg – the tibia and fibula – are fused into a single structure. As this section and the other parts of the leg straighten during a leap, huge pressures are transmitted through the bones to the heel and foot, which push off from the ground. Landing is also stressful, and the frog's short spine

absorbs a lot of the shock. The neck vertebrae are stiffened so that the heavy head does not rock around dangerously, and the rear vertebrae are fused into a long bone called the urostyle, which helps to strengthen the frog's pelvis. The pelvis is the location of the powerful leg muscles that generate most of the forward force contained in each leap.

Leaping is used primarily for escape, such as when jumping into the safety of water. Frogs cannot run, but they do walk when they want to position themselves more precisely. Walking involves moving one leg at a time on alternate sides of the body.

▷ Many poison dart frogs, such as this strawberry poison dart frog (*Oophaga pumilio*), divide their time between the ground and the trees. They are good climbers, using a hand-over-hand technique to haul themselves upward. Their toes are slightly hooked at the tip to help them grip vertical surfaces.

△ A red-eyed leaf frog (*Agalychnis callidryas*) is an agile climber. As well as making leaps between trees, it picks its way slowly through the branches, using its long, grasping fingers and toes to grip firmly.

▷ Many frogs are expert swimmers, using their webbed hind feet as paddles. Yellow-bellied toads not only use webbed feet for swimming, but also beat them in deep water to create waves pulses. Scientists believe that these wave pulses attract females.

△ A young edible frog (*Rana esculenta*) paddles through underwater vegetation using its large, webbed hind feet.

△ A marsh frog swims at the surface of the water, using all its legs to move along.

A marsh frog (*Rana ridibunda*) at full stretch as it leaps into water. The frog closes its eyes while leaping and draws them down into its mouth cavity for safety.

A giant leaf frog, or walking tree frog (*Phyllomedusa bicolor*), makes its way through a Peruvian rainforest. As its name suggests, this species and other members of the *Phyllomedusa* genus rarely jump but walk – very slowly.

△ A toad, *Oreophrynella leucomelas*, from Venezuela, is able to clamber over stones because its front and back legs are of similar length.

△ *Phyllomedusa lemur*, or the lemur leaf frog, walks along a vine in the Costa Rican rainforest.

◁ Hopping is not a very precise method of moving. Fortunately, this strawberry poison dart frog (*Oophaga pumilio*) can creep over a rock to reach a specific spot.

◁ A flying frog takes to the air. Every "flight" is an extended hop: webbed hands and feet catch the air, preventing the frog from falling too fast. Each glide is always a downward journey, but even so, large flying frogs can travel a horizontal distance of 70 m.

△ This *Rhacophorus pardalis* has landed on a fungus on the forest floor. It spends much of its time high up in the trees, gliding from branch to branch.

NIGHT VERSUS DAY

Most frogs are nocturnal, or active during the night. The obvious advantages of this behaviour is that the frogs can stay hidden in the darkness. In the rainforest, frogs' insect prey is also most active at night.

Frogs are so-called "cold-blooded" animals, but a more correct term is ectothermic, which means that a frog has no metabolic control over its body temperature. Instead, its temperature matches that of its surroundings.

Night-time temperatures in tropical areas are rarely much lower than those during the day. This makes nocturnal life viable all year around. However, in other habitats, such as mountain forests and more temperate regions, nights are considerably cooler. This restricts a frog's activities to the spring and summer. At colder times of the year frogs are inactive, both night and day.

Like other ectotherms, frogs regulate their body temperature through behaviour. Many temperate species, including the European common frog, are not entirely inactive on summer days: they bask in the sun to warm up and head into the shade or slip into water when they need to cool off.

△ Even at night, rainforests are not completely devoid of light. These toadstools from Borneo glow in the dark. They emit light constantly, but it is only visible in darkness.

◁ An Asian tree frog out hunting in the dark of the night. Its pupils are opened wide so that its eyes can collect as much light as possible.

△ A pair of edible frogs (*Rana esculenta*) mate in a shallow pool under the cover of darkness.

Many unrelated groups of frogs are active during the day. These include the mantellas and poison dart frogs. These toxic frogs rely on daylight to expose their bright colours as a warning to predators; it also makes it easier for mates to locate each other. A few harlequin toads (*Atelopus spumarius barbotini*, pictured right) are also poisonous, and they and their harmless relatives are also diurnal. During the breeding season, many other species are so busy that they are active at all times of the day and night.

△ A painted mantella (*Mantella madagascariensis*)

△ Reticulated poison dart frog (*Ranitomeya reticulata*)

△ Common toads mate in daylight at the height of the breeding season.

Like frogs, I'm often active at night. But not all of my work is done in rainforests; I have spent many nights frogging in my home country of Switzerland. In the early springtime I often go out at night to search for nocturnal mating frogs, such as the European tree frog. It is still quite cool at this time of year, especially in the water – I have to sit in it for hours on end.

When frogs are croaking they can be a bit shy, so I need to take my time. I usually use my left hand to focus the camera lens and hold a torch; I take the pictures with my right. For many years I didn't have a car and I had to go home after that cold, wet, and dirty "bath" by bicycle.

▷ A male European tree frog (*Hyla arborea*) calls by night in a pool in Switzerland.

△ These photographs show the same species of tree frog, *Hyla rubracyla*. The picture on the left was taken during the day. By night, the frog takes on a much darker colour, as seen on the right. Darker skin absorbs heat better than light skin. The change is controlled by three types of skin cells that shrink and swell to alter the proportion of different colours in the skin.

△ Frogs sleep during the day. Most hide away from view but some, such as this Asian tree frog, bed down in the open.

▷ A *Rhacophorus* species sleeps on a leaf with its long legs tucked under its body. Its upper and lower eyelids do not close completely, which means the frog remains alert for predators even while sleeping.

△ The same *Rhacophorus* species as pictured on the right, recently woken up by the camera.

CAMOUFLAGE

Adult frogs have many predators. In forests they are preyed upon by snakes, which kill with lightning-quick bites and fast-acting venom. Along river banks they are at risk from hunters such as otters or herons. Away from water, toads can fall victim to badgers and hedgehogs. Frogs may be able to leap to safety at the last minute, but not being noticed at all is a much better survival strategy. The most common method used for this purpose is camouflage.

Most predators probably detect frogs by smell, but that is usually not enough to pinpoint their victims precisely, so they switch to the sense of sight, scanning their surroundings for any typical frog shapes. The aim of camouflage is to break up that shape so it cannot be distinguished from the background. For this reason, many frogs have a "disruptive" pattern of greens and browns, similar to military fatigues. The mix of colours makes it difficult to see where a frog ends and its surroundings begin. Most frogs are able to tinker with these colours, turning them lighter and darker to match the colours around them more closely.

▷ A young European common frog (*Rana temporaria*) is hard to spot among the greens and browns of fallen leaves as it looks for a place to spend the winter.

△ A South American tree frog hides in the knot of a tree, pretending to be the pale heartwood.

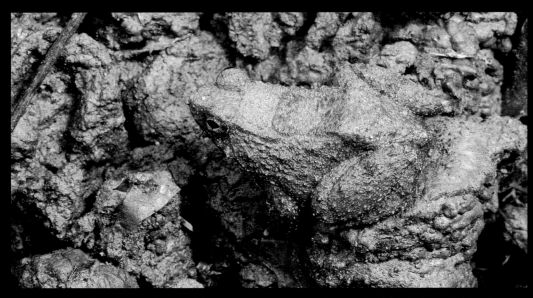

△ A seep frog (*Occidozyga baluensis*) from Borneo is covered in mud, which helps it to blend in with its environment as it waits to ambush worms and insects.

"" Frogs are not always happy to be photographed. After a few shots they usually leap away and disappear. This tree frog, however, wasn't so shy of the camera. I found it asleep on a tattered leaf. It woke after I had taken a few shots, but didn't hop away immediately. Instead, we just looked at each other for a few seconds. Then I decided to leave the frog in peace and headed off into the woodland to find other specimens. ""

▷ With its legs tucked up next to its body, this tree frog no longer looks like a frog at all. Its speckled white pattern makes it look like a bird dropping on a leaf.

▽ The tree frog, sleeping in the Llanos region of Venezuela, is roused from its sleep.

◁ A sleeping tree frog is almost perfectly camouflaged against a moonlit rock in Canaima National Park in Venezuela.

△ The camouflage illusion is shattered as soon as the frog raises its head and opens its eyes.

shapes are a very important tool in creating good camouflage. The bat-faced toad (*Bufo typhonius*) of French Guiana is a good example of a species that makes use of all three elements. On the forest floor, the pale stripe running down the back of the toad looks like the central rib of a leaf.

◁ The flattened body of the crested forest toad (*Bufo margaritifer*) has a jagged fringe. This disrupts the shape of the animal, making it appear more like a leaf than a frog.

▽ Seen from the side, the crested forest toad's ridges are visible. These are flat and curved to make it blend in among the drying, crumpled leaves on the forest floor.

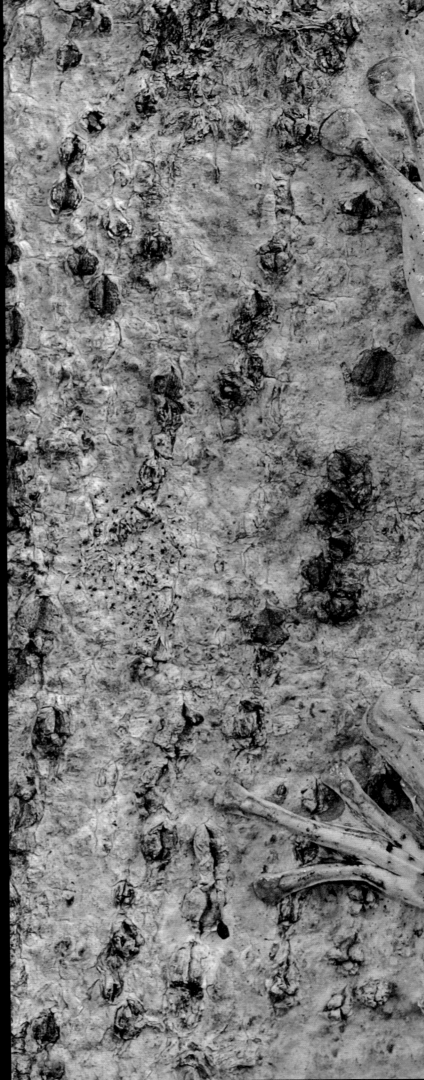

▷ Shadows are a big give-away. A frog can have excellent camouflage, but a shadow cast beneath its body is enough to highlight its shape and alert predators to its location. The file-eared tree frog (*Polypedates otilopus*) holds its body very close to a tree trunk; this ensures that any shadows are kept to a minimum throughout the day.

△ Whipping frogs (genus *Polypedates*) have flattened bodies so that they can get as close as possible to a tree trunk or similar resting place.

USING POISONS

Many types of frogs use poisons to defend themselves. The giant leaf frog (*Phyllomedusa bicolor*) of South America, for example, produces a wax containing powerful poisons. The toxic wax is secreted onto the skin by the same glands used in other species to keep their skins damp. If ingested by humans, the wax induces hallucinations: precisely why it is used by Amazonian people during religious ceremonies. They believe the trance the frog toxins produce allows shamans to communicate with spirits.

The most familiar toxic frogs are the poison dart frogs. Famously the source of the paralyzing poisons that coat the tips of arrows and hunting darts, poison dart frogs are also known for being the most brightly coloured frog species. Most do not produce particularly potent toxins; eating one will not kill a predator, but it will make it violently sick. The unfortunate predator soon learns to associate the event with the taste and colours of that type of frog: it will not eat anything that looks similar again.

Thus the death of one frog serves to protects the rest of the population.

The same strategy is used by the mantellas of Madagascar. They are brightly coloured, which warns off potential predators – yet not all frogs are telling the truth. Two harlequin toads (genus *Atelopus*) also have toxic skin. They are brightly coloured, but so are the non-toxic members of the genus. The harmless frogs mimic the warning colours of their relatives so that they look just as dangerous.

◁ The skin of the strawberry poison dart frog (*Oophaga pumilio*) contains a poison called pumiliotoxin. This substance is extremely toxic in large concentrations. However, only very small amounts are present in the frog's skin, which is not enough kill most animals. Nonetheless, just touching the skin will produce a painful rash.

△ A green mantella (*Mantella viridis*) has the same toxins in its skin as poison dart frogs, despite being totally unrelated and living in completely different parts of the world.

△ The Chocoan harlequin toad (*Atelopus spurrelli*) shares the bright colours of many other members in its genus. However, only two *Atelopus* species produce significant toxins: the Panamanian golden frog (*A. zeteki*) and variable harlequin toad (*A. varius*) produce the same deadly poison found in pufferfish.

△ The golden mantella's (*Mantella aurantiaca*) vibrant colours mark it out as an unpleasant, perhaps deadly, meal.

Toxin-producing members of the poison dart frog family exhibit a wealth of colour patterns – which in at least one case can be transferred to another species. The dyeing poison dart frog (*Dendrobates tinctorius*, pictured below) from South America is used by forest people to dye pet parrots. The frog's skin is rubbed on the skin of parrot chicks, and amazingly, the poisons cause the young birds to grow feathers in a range of colours.

△ Cauca poison frog (*Dendrobates bombetes*)

△ Harlequin poison dart frog (*Oophaga histrionica*)

△ Dyeing poison dart frog (*Dendrobates tinctorius*)

△ Reticulated poison dart frog (*Ranitomeya reticulata*)

△ The blue form of the Dyeing poison dart frog (*Dendrobates tinctorius*)

" One of the easier things about photographing poisonous frogs is that even the most toxic ones pose little danger to me. This is not always the case with other rainforest animals. One time in Sumatra, Indonesia, I hired a local guide to take me to good places to find wildlife. There were many things I wanted to see. As well as frogs, I hoped to find the rare lantern bug.

Much of the forest in Sumatra has been modified by people and much of it exists in small patches. We had been hiking for a while inside the island's Gunung Leuser National Park, one of the few places where there is still some virgin forest, when we suddenly heard a very loud roaring not far away. It sounded like a huge animal, and I asked my guide if there was a tiger nearby. I couldn't think of anything else living in a rainforest that could make such a noise.

The guide agreed it must be a tiger – one that didn't sound very friendly. I was very excited but naturally a bit frightened at the same time. My curiosity won, and I asked the guide to get me close enough to see a wild tiger in its habitat. He refused. "No way," he said. "We'd better leave immediately." I was very disappointed, but it was probably the right thing to do. Today, though, I still wonder what would have happened if we'd got close enough to take a look. "

△ Granulated poison dart frog (*Oophaga granulifera*)

△ Harlequin poison dart frog (*Oophaga histrionica*)

△ Lehmann's poison frog (*Oophaga lehmanni*)

▷ The golden poison dart frog
(*Phyllobates terribilis*) of Colombia
produces the most toxic substances
of any frog – in fact, it is the most
poisonous vertebrate of all. An
average member of this species
has 1 mg of batrachotoxin in its
skin: enough to kill 10,000 mice
or about ten people. However, the
frog is only a real danger to humans
if its toxic secretions make it into
the bloodstream through broken
skin. The toxin is made from similar
poisons harvested from termites,
ants, and other rainforest insects.
A poison dart frog raised in captivity
on non-poisonous insects will be
harmless. Batrachotoxin acts on
the nervous system, paralyzing
the muscles. If the dose is high
enough, the toxin will eventually
stop the heart.

▷ This tree frog species (*Hyloscirtus tigrinus*) was recently discovered in Colombia. It is not currently considered to be toxic, but its green and black colouring is similar to that of the green and black poison dart frog (pictured below). The poison dart species lives in the same region of Colombia as the tree frog, although it is generally restricted to forests at lower altitudes. Little is known about the tree frog, but its colouring could be mimicking the poisonous frog in an attempt to scare off predators. Alternatively, the stripes are reported to work as good camouflage, so it is just as possible that the vibrant colours of the poison dart species began as a camouflage pattern.

△ The green and black poison dart frog (*Dendrobates auratus*) is one of the most common poison dart frogs.

▷ The warts of these common toads (*Bufo bufo*) are easy to see as they mate in water. These warts are filled with a milky liquid that leaks or sprays out when a toad is handled roughly. The milk contains bufagin: a powerful steroid. High concentrations of bufagin cause heart palpitations, but only the milky fluid of cane toads (*Chaunus marinus*) is powerful enough to affect humans.

△ The fire salamander produces a powerful toxin called samandarin. This species can squirt the poison at attackers from skin glands. If the poison gets in the eyes, it causes convulsions and dangerously high blood pressure.

△ Like other members of the genus *Bufo*, the green toad (*Bufo viridis*) of southern Europe has large bulges behind the eyes. These are parotid glands: modified salivary

The veined tree frog (*Trachycephalus venulosus*) of Peru exudes a sticky white substance onto its skin. This milky froth contains an alkaloid that causes stinging if it gets into an attacker's eyes.

LAST LINE OF DEFENCE

No matter how hard a frog tries to avoid predators, the evolutionary "arms race" between hunter and hunted ensures that the predators will find potential victims on a regular basis. Once discovered, a last-ditch attempt at leaping into the safety of water or undergrowth may pay off, but it may well not be enough.

Several groups of frogs have invested in an additional insurance policy. One of the most successful strategies is to be toxic – or at least, unpleasant to eat. One bad experience and a predator quickly learns to leave similar frogs alone.

Another defence employed by some species is an armoury of prickles and spines that make them, at best, fairly uncomfortable to eat. The helmeted water toad (*Caudiverbera caudiverbera*) of Chile has developed an even more pro-active approach. At up to 25 cm long, it is a large frog that preys on birds, fish, and lizards. At that size, it makes a good meal, and its predators include humans, who prize its meat. When threatened, the toad inflates its lungs so that its body swells to maximum size, then it rears up on its hind legs and lunges, mouth open, at its attackers. That is usually enough to scare off predators.

△ This Colombian toad of the genus *Bufo* is equipped with spined crests behind its eyes – which make it an unpleasant item to swallow.

◁ The red-eyed leaf frog (*Agalychnis callidryas*) has bands of bright colours along its flanks. Usually hidden by the thighs when the frog is perched on a branch, the colours are exposed as a bright flash when the frog's legs extend during a leap. The change from green to multiple colours requires a predator to adjust the way it tracks the frog as it leaps. When the frog lands and tucks it bright flanks away again, to the predator's eyes, it has effectively disappeared.

△ The file-eared tree frog (*Polypedates otilophus*) is named after sharp extensions on its jaw bone. These lie beneath the skin but jab painfully into anything that tries to pick the frog up.

The tomato frog (*Dyscophus antongilli*) exudes goo from its skin. When a predator bites the frog, the goo gums up the attacker's mouth; the sticky liquid also spreads across its face, gluing its eyes closed – so that the frog can escape unseen.

UNWANTED COMPETITION

Most frogs are specialists. This is especially true of the frogs that inhabit the world's rainforests and are part of wildlife communities that have remained undisturbed for millions of years. Each species has evolved to exist in an intricate and delicately balanced web of life. If organisms – whether animals, plants, or fungi – are introduced from outside the ancient ecosystem, indigenous rainforest frogs can be put at risk.

Perhaps the worst offenders are other frog species. Several have evolved generalist lifestyles, which allow them to survive in a range of habitats. These include many types of toad and the bullfrogs. In the past century, a number of these species have been spread around the world by people: some by accident, others by design. The adaptable behaviour of the new arrivals meant that they survived wherever they ended up – often at the expense of many native frogs.

The African clawed frog (*Xenopus laevis*) was one species deliberately imported by humans into various countries around the world. These frogs are sensitive to human pregnancy hormones and were once used for primitive pregnancy tests. However, the African frogs also carry a fungus; they are immune to it, but it caused other frog species to develop a deadly disease called chytridiomycosis. Within the last decade, the fungus has been found in most parts of the world. It is thought to be the force behind a global reduction in frog numbers that has left 30 per cent of frog species under threat of extinction.

△ Cane toads (*Chaunus marinus*) were introduced to Australia from the Americas in 1935. They were meant to control a beetle that was damaging sugar cane crops. However, soon the fast-breeding toads became an even worse pest. The 101 original toads have now multiplied into 200 million individuals.

◁ American bullfrogs (*Rana catesbeiana*) are native to eastern North America. However, they have been introduced to the west of that continent, Central and South America, and Europe. The pictured individual is in Colombia, where it is able to dominate smaller species. Bullfrogs are thought to be one of the species that is spreading *Batrachochytrium dendrobatidis*, the fungus behind chytridiomycosis, across South America – to devastating effect.

△ The cayenne stubfoot toad (*Atelopus flavescens*), a harlequin frog from French Guiana, is one of the South American species threatened by chytridiomycosis.

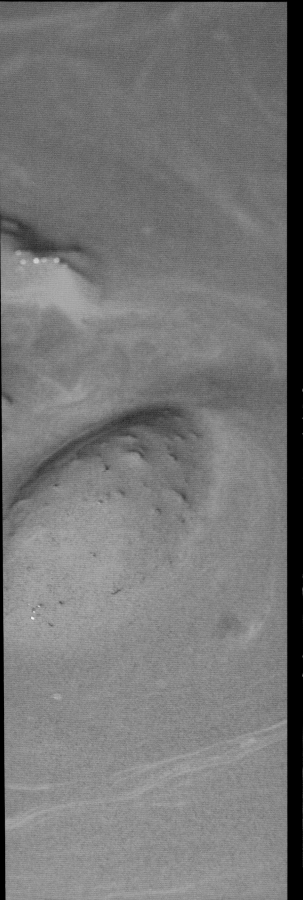

❝ You never know when you might come across a frog. While travelling one night in Madagascar, I came across this African bullfrog living in a muddy puddle in the middle of the road. This is a good example of how certain species are able to survive more or less anywhere. ❞

◁ The African bullfrog (*Pyxicephalus adspersus*) has been introduced to Madagascar. There are fears that this species will do more damage to the island's already threatened natural wildlife. It is also possible that the incomer has introduced chytridiomycosis.

△ Photographer Thomas Marent in action in Madagascar, photographing the African bullfrog seen left.

reproduction

breeding behaviour

The only time frogs pay attention to each other is when it is time
to breed, and then the race is on to find the best mates.

A frog starts its life in water and needs
to undergo a remarkable transformation
before it is able to move onto land.
Of course, this process has its advantages
and disadvantages. Among the benefits is
the fact that young and adults are not in
direct competition with each other for
resources. Tadpoles live in a completely
different habitat from their parents and
have an independent food source; this
means that the number of tadpoles
produced by a pair of frogs does not

impact on the survival of the adults.
As a result, the average frog pair can
afford to produce hundreds, if not
thousands, of eggs. While not competing
with their parents, the sheer number
of offspring means that there are not
enough resources for so many, and only
the strongest – and most fortunate –
survive into adulthood.

The big disadvantage of a frog's
dependence on water is that few species
can breed away from it. This, for the

△ A froglet of a European tree frog (*Hyla
arborea*) has four legs and a tail. ▷ A male and
female Australian red-eyed tree frog (*Litoria
chloris*) in amplexus: the mating posture in
which the male clings to the female's back.

most part, excludes them from drier
habitats. Frogs do survive in arid
conditions, but in such cases they form
only a small part of the ecosystem. Damp,
humid places suit the frog breeding
system best – and allow them to thrive.

LIFE CYCLE

Most frogs emerge from their eggs as legless, tailed, fish-like tadpoles that live and breathe in water. As they develop, they grow legs, lose their gills – developing lungs instead – and gradually re-absorb their tails into their bodies. The end result is a froglet: a tiny frog that begins its life on land.

Despite outward appearances, this process is not that far removed from the development of other vertebrates. Land vertebrates from frogs to mammals progress through a similar sequence of forms. All vertebrate embryos, including those of humans, have gill slits, or clefts, in their necks during their early development. The difference is that most of the development of birds, lizards, mammals, or indeed, people is hidden from view within an egg or inside the mother, while amphibian embryos become independent while still in a form that breathes with gills. The subsequent development of lungs and limbs occurs during the frog's tadpole phase; lizards, birds, and mammals do this as embryos.

The pictures over the next six pages show the various stages in the growth of a European common frog (*Rana temporaria*) – from egg to adult.

▷ The frog life cycle begins with mating. Male and female frogs produce sex cells, each of which contain a half set of chromosomes. When a male sperm fuses with a female egg, it creates a single cell with a complete set of DNA. The fertilized egg, or zygote, then rapidly divides in a process known as a mitosis to become an embryo.

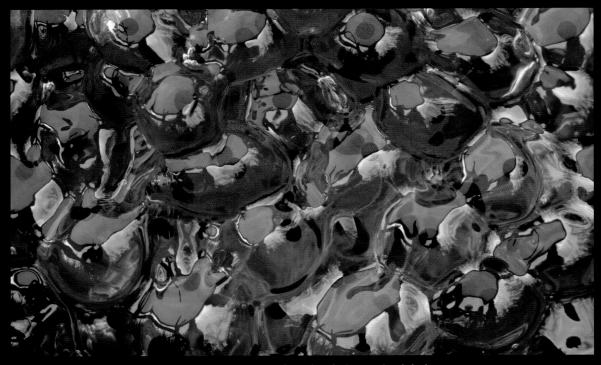

△ Like other cold-water species, European common frogs lay their eggs in globular masses of jelly. In warm water, frogs tend to lay thin mats of eggs instead.

called the urostyle. This bone is
inside the frog's rump and provides
structural support for the pelvis.

REPRODUCTION

△ Tiny tadpoles hatch from the eggs after a few weeks.

△ At first, the tadpole's body is almost spherical.

△ The back legs are the first pair to emerge.

△ The back legs are well formed by the time the frong legs develop.

▷ Three or four months after being laid as a fertilized egg, the young frog is strong enough to leave the water and seek out a dark and damp place in which to hibernate through the winter. The following spring, it will concentrate on feeding and growing. It is unlikely that this individual will mate successfully until the age of three.

△ The tapole has now become a tail-less froglet. This one is no more than a couple of centimetres long and still spends a lot of time in water.

As is common in the animal kingdom, it is up to male frogs to attract mates. They do this by producing loud calls. These vary from species to species, ranging from deep croaks to high-pitched chirps and buzzes.

A call is produced by a voicebox, or larynx, which contains muscle fibres that vibrate when air is forced over them to produce a distinctive sound. Both male and female frogs have voiceboxes, but only the male has muscle fibres large enough to produce loud calls. Many, but by no means all, male frogs also inflate a balloon of skin on the throat, called the vocal sac, while calling. This helps to transmit the sound from the larynx into the air.

It is sometimes suggested that deeper calls attract more mates. However, studies have shown that males that call most frequently are the most attractive to females. An interested female will then hop towards the calls of her chosen mate, pausing every now and then to be sure she is heading in the right direction. A large male will do his best to ensure that he is the only caller in the area by bullying smaller males away. However, some males choose to stay silent and creep up close to where the big male is performing. When a prospective mate approaches through the darkness, the silent male intercepts her and jumps on her back, ready to begin mating.

REPRODUCTION

△ Stripeless tree frogs (*Hyla meridionalis*) make a deep "cra-a-ar" call. This resonant call can be heard many kilometres away during the peak of the breeding season.

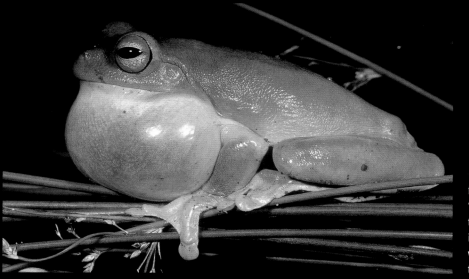

◁ The Australian red-eyed tree frog (*Litoria chloris*) makes an "ark-ark" call. The vocal sac helps to broadcast the call and also introduces harmonic frequencies, which make the call travel further through the forest.

△ A male common frog croaks in water. The huge vocal sac works like the sounding board of a piano or diaphragm of a loudspeaker. The inflated sac does not add energy to the call, but vibrates in the air to transmit sound waves in front of the frog.

◁ Male Lesueur's frogs (*Litoria lesueurii*) from Australia produce soft, purring calls. Despite being a tree frog, this species lives on the ground. Males gather in large numbers beside shallow streams at warm times of the year. Such choruses are most often heard after rainfall.

◁ At 13 cm long, the white-lipped tree frog (*Litoria infrafrenata*) of Australia is the world's largest tree frog species. This male is making its presence felt by calling from a prominent perch. Its mating calls are loud barks, although both sexes in this species also produce quieter mews when in distress.

△ *Cochranella truebae*, a glass frog, calls in the misty cloud forest of Peru. As is typical of glass frogs, this species produces whistling calls.

The marsh frog (*Rana ridibunda*) has two vocal sacs, a feature shared with other so-called water frogs, a subgroup of the genus *Rana*, which also includes the pool frog (*R. lessonae*) and the edible frog (*R. esculenta*). Marsh frogs produce a "brek-keh-kek" call.

◁ A marsh frog (*Rana ridibunda*) produces a call that sounds like "brek-keh-kek". Hybrid female edible frogs (*R. esculenta*) – the offspring of a union between *R. ridibunda* and the pool frog (*R. lessonae*) – may respond to this call and mate with a male marsh frog. If edible frogs mate with each other, however, their offspring rarely survive due to a fault in the hybrid's sex cells.

△ Natterjack toads are said to be the loudest amphibians in Europe. The scraping, rachet-like call can be heard several kilometres away. People have even mistaken a chorus of toads for a passing train.

When I visited the lowland rainforest of Borneo, I wanted to find the black-spotted rock frog, which has interesting courtship behaviour. They only live beside waterfalls, and the males attract the females by lifting up their hind limbs instead of calling. The scientists at the research centre recommended that I go with a guide because the trails to the small waterfall where I could find this species were not well marked. Unfortunately, no guide was available, so I decided to go by myself.

It was a difficult hike. The forest floor was covered with leeches, which gave me painful bites, but much more annoying were the horseflies that buzzed around my head. I had a small map and knew that I had to follow a big river to get to the frogs' waterfall. Once I arrived I found the very shy rock frogs and saw the males' displays. However, every time I tried to get close, they jumped into the water. Finally, I managed to take a few shots, and then it was time to hike out of the forest.

Suddenly, it began pouring with rain and a lightning storm blew up. I passed another research group down the trail. One of the members told me that I should not be out in the forest in this kind of weather, and they headed off in the opposite direction. That puzzled me. Where were they going in this weather? Then I realized that I must be hiking in the wrong direction. I turned around, but by now the others had disappeared in the rain.

I kept hiking until almost dusk and eventually I began to panic. I thought, "Please don't get lost in the forest again!" It had happened twice before, and I just knew that the leeches and the mosquitos were going to suck my blood all night long. I had no food and water, my little map was soaked through, and I couldn't make out the trails any more. I hoped the people at the centre would come looking for me if I didn't arrive back by nightfall. I was crazy enough to take a picture of myself at this point: I looked awful. But I didn't give up and decided to take a different route, finding my way by torch. It was almost a miracle that this trail led me back to the research centre. I was near exhaustion once I finally arrived. 🙶🙷

The black-spotted rock frog (*Staurois natator*) lives beside noisy waterfalls. Males do call, but because they may not be heard above the roar of the falls, they also use a visual signal called "foot flagging" to attract mates. This involves raising their hind legs to reveal a patch of pale-blue skin around the top of the inner thigh.

MATING

Although it may often look like it, frogs do not copulate, or mate internally. Instead, they form an amplexus. This term is derived from the Latin word for "embrace", and that is exactly what it is. The male climbs onto the back of a receptive female and clings on tightly. The female then begins to deposit her eggs, and the male immediately spreads his sperm over them. Fertilization, in which an egg and sperm combine to make a genetically unique individual, therefore takes place outside of the body. Amplexus may last minutes or several hours, depending on the species.

Frog species that live in the humid tropics are able to breed all year round. The process of calling and mating is a continuous one, although it is often most prolific after a rain shower, when conditions are ideal for the eggs. Species living in more restrictive habitats, such as those that experience winters or droughts, have only a few opportunities to breed each year – perhaps just one.

When conditions are favourable, an entire population of frogs will try to breed. This results in an explosion of activity, with a mass movement of frogs to breeding sites, males calling in immense choruses, and intense – often violent – competition for mates. While tropical species have time to attract mates through calling, the "explosive" breeders are much more desperate: males will grab anything that moves, including other males as well as females from other species.

Explosive breeders tend to return to the same pond or body of water in which they were tadpoles. The smell remembered from their younger days undoubtedly helps adult frogs identify their home pools, but they also probably simply remember where it is.

◁ A pair of barred leaf frogs (*Phyllomedusa tomopterna*) in amplexus. Tree frogs like these and other species that evolved relatively recently have a forward amplexus, in which the male holds on to his mate's upper arms and armpits.

△ Two male rain frogs (genus *Eleutherodactylus*) try to mate with a female. The upper male is unlikely to have much success.

△ A male dainty green tree frog keeps calling while mating. The call discourages rival males from approaching.

◁ Poison dart frogs, including the golden species (*Phyllobates terribilis*), can mate as often as once a month. They employ a range of amplexus postures. This pair is using a basic abdominal grip, in which the male grasps the female by the belly rather than underneath the armpits. On other occasions the pair might use cephalic amplexus where the male holds the female by the head.

◁ The amplexus of European common frogs (*Rana temporaria*) usually takes place in water.

▷ However, competiton for mates is enormous during the breeding season, and males often ambush females before they have made it to the breeding pool. This strategy is not always a good one because the eggs fertilized during mating could dry out on the river bank.

▽ These pebas stubfoot toads (*Atelopus pumarius barbotini*) are sexual athletes. Once a male positions himself on a mate, he will not let go until he has fertilized as many eggs as possible, which means amplexus may go on for several days or even weeks. The male secretes sticky mucus that glues his belly to his mate's back. Eggs and sperm are not produced continuously, however; instead, they are deposited in several clutches.

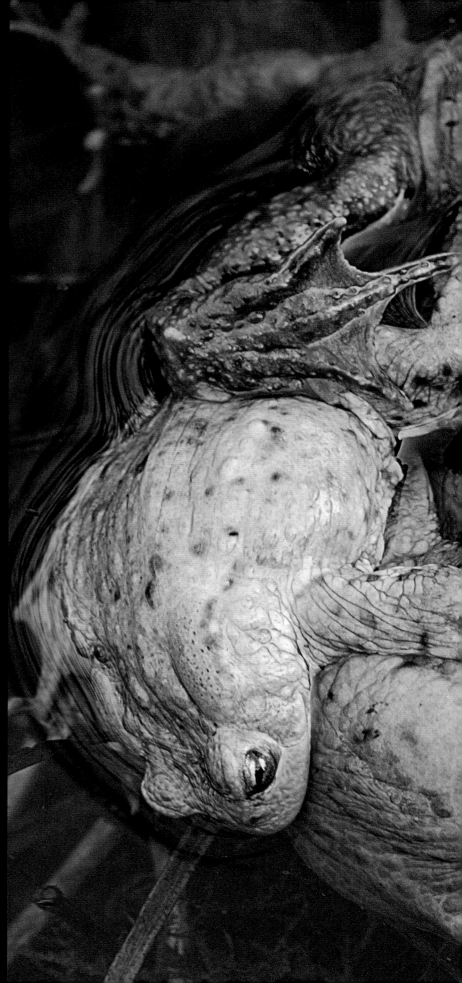

▷ Somewhere in the middle of this ball of male common toads (*Bufo bufo*) is a female. She has little control over who will win the battle to be her mate. It is not uncommon for a female trapped inside a toad ball to drown while the males are busy fighting over her.

This male toad is lucky to have found an available mate. A large female like this will produce about 5,000 eggs.

Laliostoma labrosum, a common species from Madagascar, mates on the floor of dry forests. The small fertilized eggs are laid in puddles and stagnant pools.

SEXUAL DIFFERENCES

Many species of frog exhibit something called sexual dimorphism, which simply means that males and females do not look alike. For example, it is common for one sex to be larger than the other. In tropical species with a continuous breeding season, females are often the larger sex, which allows them to produce large numbers of eggs. However, males of seasonally breeding species, such as bullfrogs and toads, tend to be the larger.

This is because these males must compete harder — even fight — for access to mates. In general, smaller males are unable to mate at all.

In some instances, the only way to tell a male from a female is to look for "nuptial pads". These areas of thickened skin on the side of a male frog's first finger are most obvious during the mating season, because their role is to help males hold on to their mates.

▷ This male white-lipped tree frog (*Litoria infrafrenata*) is bright green to ensure potential mates can see him. The female has taken on more cryptic camouflage colours so that she can stay out of sight. This is a good example of the different needs of males and females belonging to the same species.

△ This pair of European common frogs (*Rana temporaria*) look like they might be different species. However, red-brown individuals are not unusual, and the males sometimes turn blue in the mating season.

▷ This male tomato frog (*Dyscophus antongilii*) is considerably smaller than its mate. However, this is no disadvantage. Making eggs requires a lot more energy than making sperm, so the smaller male can easily produce enough sperm to cover the eggs released by his mate.

△ Eggs ready for fertilization are clearly visible in the swollen
belly of this female walking tree frog, (*Phyllomedusa palliata*)
from Peru.

SPAWN

Frog spawn is the name given to the masses of jelly-like eggs that are left behind after mating is over. Generally these are floating in water or glued to plants. Huge numbers of these eggs are preyed upon by fish against which they have no protection. Some species lay their eggs in the relative safety of an underground nest or deposit them on the branches that overhang water.

Unlike the eggs of reptiles or birds, frog eggs do not have a waterproof coat or shell. Instead the embryo develops inside a ball of jelly. This makes it prone to drying out and gives little protection from infection or parasites. The eggs laid outside of water might be safe from fish, but the parents often have to expend a lot of time and resources ensuring their growing eggs are keep moist and clean.

△ A pair of European common frogs mate in water that is brimming with the frog spawn left by other couples. This female will add about another 2,000 eggs to the collection.

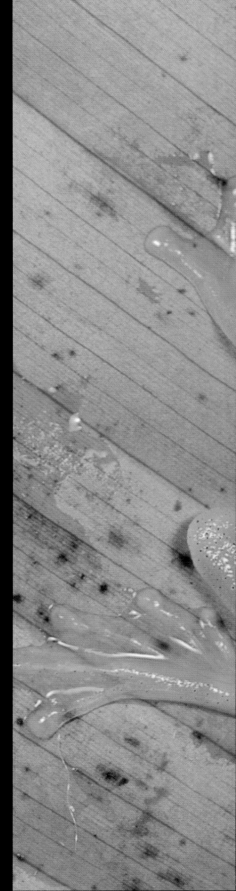

▷ A female Fleischmann's glass frog (*Hyalinobatrachium fleischmanni*) tends to her eggs on a leaf. She returns to them regularly to provide a protective coat of mucus. This keeps the eggs moist and also supplies protection from fungus and parasites.

△ The heads and tails of developing tadpoles are clearly visible inside these eggs.

◁ Whipping frogs, such as this species, *Otilophus polypedates*, from Borneo, are named for the way they whip up foam nests with their back legs.

▽ Great grey tree frogs (*Chiromantis xerampelina*) make a large foam nest. Several males help a female do this by frothing up a mixture of mucus and air. The female lays eggs in the soft foam, and the males tussle to add their sperm to the mix. The foam then hardens to form a protective case around the eggs. The nests hang on branches above water. When the eggs hatch, the tadpoles break out of the foam and fall into the water to continue development.

△ A grasshopper nymph visits a blob of spawn laid on a leaf in Madagascar. Once the tiny tadpoles developing inside are old enough, they will drip into a pool of water below.

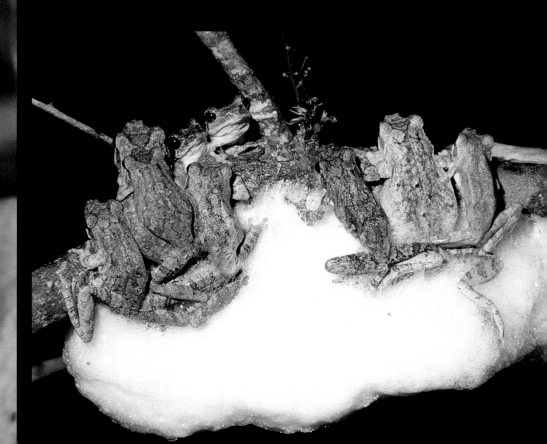

his back. He will take them to a
larger pool, where they will be
able to feed themselves.

△ The eggs of the golden poison dart frog (*Phyllobates terribilis*) develop in a tiny puddle on
a leaf. The bulbous part of the embryo is a yolk sac, which contains a supply of nutrients.

Male midwife toads (*Alytes obstetricans*) are in charge of the eggs, often carrying those of several mates. After guarding them in a burrow for seven to eight weeks, the male then transports his eggs to water, where they can hatch into tadpoles.

to develop into tadpoles. Once hatched, tadpoles have but one purpose: to eat and grow. Tadpoles generally take no more than a month or two to make the change into a frog; the precise period largely depends on water temperature and the availability of food. However, some frog species pause in the tadpole phase, only transforming into adults months or even years later.

The best example of this is the paradox frog (*Pseudis paradoxa*), one of seven South American species classified in a family all their own.

way its tadpoles spend more than a year growing to a length of 25 cm. When they finally make the transition into adult form, they become frogs that are perhaps a third of this size.

How can a juvenile animal be larger than the adult it turns into? The answer in this case lies in the tail. Most frogs continue to grow once they have metamorphosed, but the body of a paradox frog tadpole is the same size as the adult. The reduction in size is simply a result of the tadpole's tail being re-absorbed into the frog's body.

△ When it hatches, a tadpole has feathery external gills. However, within a few days these have been encased in fold of skin called an operculum.

◁ Most tadpoles are plant eaters. They eat microscopic algae or scrape mouthfuls of cells off dead plants with rows of horny strips in their mouths. Plant food takes a lot of digesting, and a tadpole has a long and highly coiled gut.

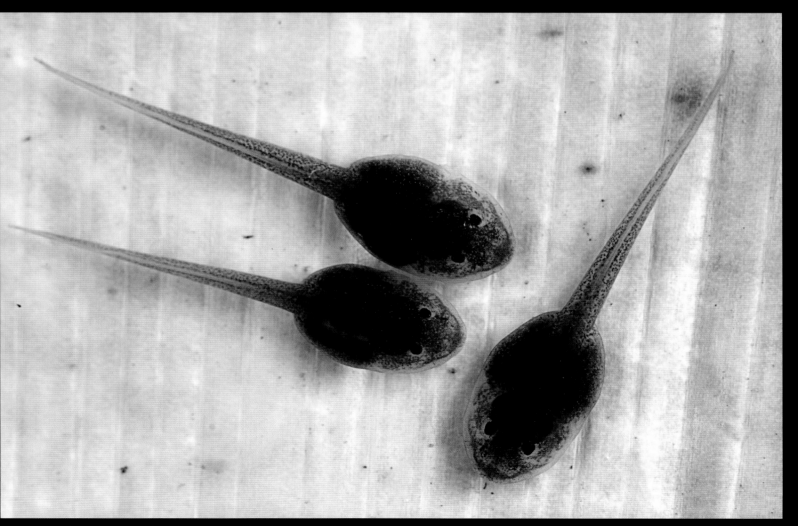

△ Golden poison dart frog (*Phyllobates terribilis*) tadpoles eat plants and algae, but they will also feast on carrion and even smaller tadpoles.

The tadpoles of most poison dart frogs spend their early life in a shallow pool. This specimen in a puddle on the forest floor is from the species *Ranitomeya reticulata*. Its mother will visit from time to time to feed her young with unfertilized eggs.

◁ Once a tadpole has grown four legs, such as this young European tree frog (*Hyla arborea*), it is able to come onto land, as its gills have almost shrivelled away and it can breathe in the air. However, having a tail is a hindrance, so the tadpole generally keeps to the water until it becomes a fully formed froglet.

▽ A young *Hyla arborea* froglet perches on a leaf. Without its tail, the froglet can now move around by hopping.

FROGLETS

Once it has lost its tail and has developed legs, a froglet still has a lot of growing up to do. Most stay close to their aquatic nursery and this is often the place where they first start to hunt for prey. In general, there is still a good deal of development to be done before a froglet can survive by itself on land.

Several groups of frogs get a head-start as froglets, gaining either much more protection in the tadpole stage, or bypassing it altogether.

One example is Darwin's frog (*Rhinoderma darwinii*) from South America. Fathers of this species scoop newly hatched tadpoles into their vocal sacs and keep them there until they are ready to emerge as froglets. The three-toed toadlets of Brazil lay eggs that hatch into miniature versions of the adults, and the rain frogs (genus *Eleutherodactylus*) also use this method of "direct development". The Puerto Rican live-bearing frog (*E. jasperi*) goes one stage further and gives birth to its froglets. Like reptiles and birds, the eggs of direct-developing frog species are stocked with large amounts of yolk to supply the growing froglets through their extended development.

▽ This unusual-looking flat species is called the Surinam toad (*Pipa pipa*). It is completely aquatic, even as an adult, and also has a unique method of raising its young. Up to 100 fertilized eggs are embedded in the skin on their mother's back. They develop there for three or four months before hatching as tiny toadlets.

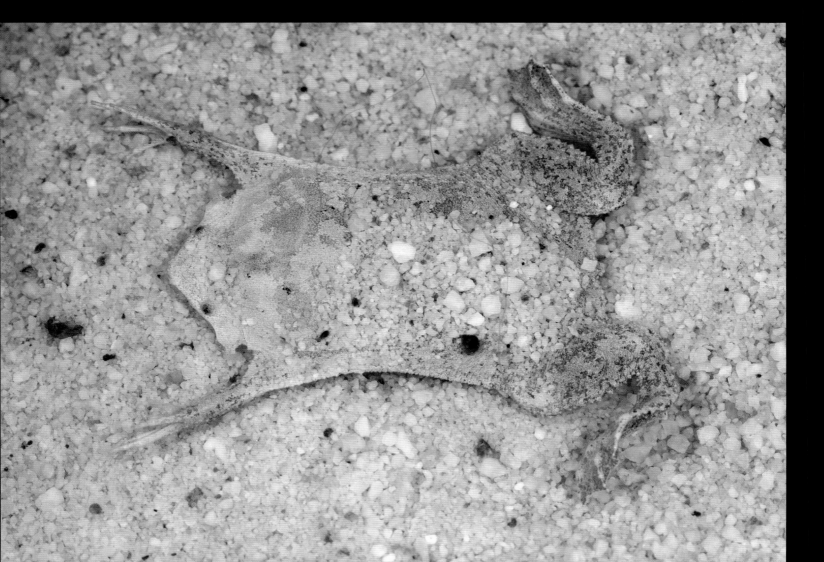

◁△ This yellow-striped poison frog
(*Dendrobates truncatus*) tadpole
will soon be a land-based froglet.
Even in this young state, the tadpole
has taken on the vibrant striped
pattern of the adult it will become.

△ Perhaps unsurprisingly
for a walking tree frog, this
Phyllomedusa bicolor tadpole
is able to take a walk on a leaf.

◁ *P. bicolor* is one of the largest
tree frogs in the world, and takes
several years to mature. This
specimen shows the spotted
pattern of a juvenile frog.

he reproductive behaviour of newts and salamanders could not be more different from that of frogs. For most of these creatures, fertilization is internal: a packet of a male's sperm is introduced into the female's reproductive opening, where it joins with the eggs while still inside her body.

The sperm is transferred during an elaborate mating ritual, which varies from species to species. These rituals rely a lot more on scent than is apparent in frog reproduction, and the odours released by the male make the female receptive to mating. Some salamander species take this a step further: a male scrapes his mate's back with his teeth, making her bleed. He then releases stimulating hormones directly into her bloodstream which turn her into a receptive partner.

Some members of this group are not true amphibians; instead, they spend their entire lives either in water or on land. As a result, their life cycle is somewhat simplified. Aquatic salamanders, such as waterdogs and mudpuppies, hatch from eggs as tadpole-like larvae. These grow into a gill-breathing adult form without altering their fundamental body shape. Terrestrial species, such as the North American salamanders, undergo direct development: their eggs hatch into miniature adults. Newts are true amphibians, however. Like frogs, they pass through an aquatic, gill-breathing stage before becoming primarily land-based animals with lungs.

△ An alpine newt (*Mesotriton alpestris*) shows off its orange underside.

▷ Only male great crested newts (*Triturus cristatus*) grow crests, and then only during the breeding season. Courtship and mating take place in water during spring and summer.

△ When she lays her eggs, the female great crested newt (*Triturus cristatus*) will wrap them in leaves for protection.

△ The male great crested's enlarged tail fin helps it compete with

▷ Male alpine newts (*Mesotriton alpestris*) do not grow pronounced crests during the mating season, but they do develop very bright colouring which helps them to stand out against water plants.

△ Female alpine newts have a similar colour pattern to that of the males, but it is not as vibrant.

▽▷ Since they hatched from their eggs, these smooth newt (*Triturus vulgaris*) larvae have breathed with feathery gills. Unlike in tadpoles, the gills remain on the outside of the body until the newts are ready to leave the water. Young newts that have recently begun a life on land are known as efts. Where water temperatures are low, newt larvae develop slowly and may not become efts for several years.

◁ The eggs of alpine newts are anchored to water plants for protection.

▽ In the same way as lungs, gills work by having as large a surface area as possible. In this respect, a newt's gills are inside-out lungs: the feathery sections are filled with blood vessels, which pick up oxygen dissolved in the water. Like frogs, newts also breathe through their skins.

Heterixalus punctatus,
Madagascar

Cochranella spinosa
glass frogs, Colombia

amphibian families

The class Amphibia has in the region of 6,000 species arranged across 46 families in three orders. Frogs and toads make up the bulk of the class. They are grouped as the order Anura, which has at least 5,550 species in 30 families. The second largest order, Caudata, has approximately 560 species in ten families. Finally, the Gymnophiona, or caecilians, make up about 170 species in six families. All the families are listed on the following three pages. The classification of amphibians is a contentious issue and one that is very much in flux, with new information about relationships, based on genetic studies, changing the picture all the time. This means that both common and scientific names often change.

Order: Anura (frogs and toads)

Key features of this group are the absence of a tail, hindlegs that are larger than the forelegs, and communication by sound. The order is divided into two unequal parts: the suborders Archaeobatrachia and Neobatrachia. These are somewhat artificial groupings: the families within each group are not necessarily closely related. In fact, some members of the Archaeobatrachia are perhaps more closely related to families in the other suborder. Biologists dislike the term "primitive" because it carries with it connotations of being inferior. Evolution does not draw such distinctions, so in that context, the two suborders divide the frogs into primitive forms and those that evolved later on. The archaeobatrachians have a form that is thought to be most similar to that of the first frogs. The name of the group means "ancients frogs". The neobatrachians – "new frogs" – have a wider range of lifestyles and anatomical features that are believed to have evolved on several occasions later on.

Suborder: Archaeobatrachia

Family: Alytidae
Common name: Midwife toads
Distribution: Western Europe and northwest Africa
Size: 5 species
Description: Terrestrial toads about 5 or 6 cm long. The male collects fertilized eggs and carries them on his back for several weeks. He keeps them moist by taking dips in pools and hiding in damp burrows.

Family: Ascaphidae
Common name: Tailed frogs
Distribution: Western North America
Size: 2 species
Description: Despite their names, tailed frogs do not have tails. Only males have the appendage, which is an extension of the cloaca. The cloaca is the frog's single rear opening through which passes sperm, faeces, and urine. The extended and flexible cloaca is used to transfer sperm to the female, making these the only frogs to employ internal fertilization. The frogs live in swift streams, and sperm and eggs would be washed way if they were being fertilized externally.

Family: Bombinatoridae
Common name: Fire-bellied toads
Distribution: Europe, and East and Southeast Asia
Size: 10 species
Description: Small, flat toads with brightly coloured bellies. They spend most of their time in warm, shallow streams. The barbourulas of Borneo and Palwan are completely aquatic. Fire-bellied toads show off their bright bellies when threatened. They raise all four legs above the body in a posture known as the "unken reflex".

Family: Discoglossidae
Common name: Painted Frogs
Distribution: Western Europe and northwest Africa
Size: 6 species
Description: Although often grouped with the midwife toads, painted frogs look less like stout toads and a lot more like slender, brightly patterned frogs. One difference with true frogs is that painted frogs have triangular or round pupils instead of horizontal ones.

Family: Leiopelmatidae
Common name: New Zealand primitive frogs
Distribution: North Island and northern South Island
Size: 4 species
Description: This isolated family shares some of the skeletal features of the tailed frogs and so is thought to have a similarly primitive form. However, the New Zealand frogs do not have a cloacal "tail", and their fertilization is external.

Family: Megophryidae
Common name: Asian toad frogs, or litter frogs
Distribution: Southeast Asia, Nepal to southern China
Size: 138 species
Description: Many of these species live beside streams. Several species have horn-like appendages above the eyes, which allow them to hide out among the plants on the stream bank or in leaf litter.

Family: Pelobatidae
Common name: Spadefoot toads
Distribution: North America, Iberia, northwest Africa, and Eastern Europe to Central Asia
Size: 11 species
Description: Sometimes divided into two families – the American spadefoots and Eurasian spadefoots – this group of frogs lives in dry areas with loose soils. The "spadefoot" name is derived from a wedge-shaped structure on the first toe of both hind feet. This is used to dig deep burrows in which to sit out droughts.

Family: Pelodytidae
Common name: Parsley frogs
Distribution: Southwest Europe and Caucasus
Size: 3 species
Description: Small, nocturnal frogs that are named after their speckled green colour. They live in coastal forests and in forested canyons drained by streams.

Family: Pipidae
Common name: Clawed frogs
Distribution: Sub-Saharan Africa, tropical South America
Size: 31 species
Description: A family of almost completely aquatic frogs. Adults can survive in air but cannot move over land unless it is very wet. They have webbed feet and scaly tips to their toes, which are used for clawing through soft sediment for food. Clawed toads do not have tongues. They produce rattling noises underwater to attract mates.

Family: Rhinophrynidae
Common name: Mexican burrowing toad
Distribution: Rio Grande Valley from Texas to Costa Rica
Size: 1 species
Description: A single burrowing species with a spade-like hind foot and a narrow head for driving through the soil. This species hunts underground, preying on termites and other small invertebrates.

Suborder: Neobatrachia

Family: Aromobatidae
Common name: Aromobatid frogs
Distribution: South and Central America
Size: 93 species
Description: Except for one nocturnal aquatic species all other members of this family are diurnal and terrestrial, with cryptic brown and grey colouration.

Family: Arthroleptidae
Common name: Squeakers and cricket frogs
Distribution: Sub-Saharan Africa
Size: 133 species
Description: Small frogs, some of which lay their eggs on the ground. These eggs hatch straight into froglets.

Family: Brachycephalidae
Common name: Three-toed toadlets, saddle-back toads
Distribution: Southeast Brazil
Size: 11 species
Description: Found only in patches of Atlantic forest in Brazil, these frogs are all threatened with extinction. They have just three toes on the hind feet and two or three on the forefeet. Eggs are laid in leaf litter and hatch into tiny froglets. There is no tadpole phase.

Family: Brevicipitidae
Common name: Rain frogs
Distribution: Eastern and southern Sub-Saharan Africa
Size: 25 species
Description: A family of fat frogs, usuallly with a burrowing lifestyle. They have a very bulbous body and very short head. The young emerge fully metamorphosed from the eggs.

Family: Bufonidae
Common name: True toads
Distribution: North America, South America, Africa, Europe, and Asia
Size: 512 species
Description: A large group of species that contains the true toads and harlequin toads (or frogs). Typical toads have dry, warty skin, and are ground-living and active at night; some, cane toads for example, grow to a large size.

Family: Centrolenidae
Common name: Glass frogs
Distribution: Central America, northern South America, and Southeast Brazil
Size: 148 species
Description: Small, green frogs that are adapted to life in trees. The frogs get their name from the thin skin, which is transparent in some places.

Family: Dendrobatidae
Common name: Poison dart frogs
Distribution: Central and South America
Size: 166 species
Description: A group of colourful little frogs, many of which secrete poisons in their skins. The poisons are derived from chemicals harvested from insect prey. Most poison dart frogs are not deadly and simply make predators sick. However, a few have very potent toxins.

Family: Heleophrynidae
Common name: Ghost frogs
Distribution: Southern Africa
Size: 6 species
Description: A family of frogs adapted to life in fast-flowing streams. During the mating season, males develop a series of spines on the body. The ghost frog tadpoles must battle against the current and have a large

tail to aid swimming. They also have large sucker-shaped mouths for clinging to smooth pebbles on the stream bed. It takes more than a year for the tadpoles to make the change into an adult.

Family: Hemisotidae
Common name: Shovel-nosed frogs
Distribution: Sub-Saharan Africa
Size: 9 species
Description: These frogs have pointed, smooth snouts and burrow into sandy soils headfirst. Mating takes place underground in a chamber beside a pool. While the male digs his way out, the female stays with the eggs until they are ready to hatch. Then she digs a tunnel to the pool and leads her young to the water.

Family: Hylidae
Common name: American and Australian tree frogs
Distribution: North America, South America, Europe, Australia, and East Asia
Size: 852 species
Description: A large group of frogs that is found across the world. Most of these species are adapted to life in the branches, with long arms and legs for climbing and jumping. The tips of the toes are flattened into pads, which provide extra grip.

Family: Hyperoliidae
Common name: African tree frogs
Distribution: Sub-Saharan Africa and Madagascar
Size: 213 species
Description: A group of medium-sized climbing frogs. They are most common in vegetation beside water. Some eggs are laid inside nests of folded leaves. Bush frogs bury their eggs beside water. When heavy rain runs into the pools, these eggs hatch and the tadpoles wriggle across the wet ground to the deep water.

Family: Leptodactylidae
Common name: Tropical frogs
Distribution: Central and South America, Florida in North America, and Caribbean islands
Size: 1347 species
Description: Currently the largest family of anurans. This is a diverse group, whose members have a wide array of survival strategies and life cycles. The family name means "thin toes". Many have long, thin and unwebbed feet, but several family members have webbed feet. The group includes the horned frogs, which are wide-mouthed ambushers, and the rain frogs, many of which undergo direct development from egg to froglet, bypassing the tadpole stage.

Family: Limnnodynastidae
Common name: Australian ground frogs
Distribution: Australia and New Guinea
Size: 49 species
Description: Many members of this family are burrowers and live in desert regions. They store water in their bodies so they can survive long periods of drought. When it rains the frogs emerge to lay eggs in the puddles. All produce free-swimming tadpoles and have to move quickly to breed before the drought returns.

Family: Mantellidae
Common name: Mantellas
Distribution: Madagascar
Size: 169 species
Description: Once thought to belong to the Hylidae and then the Rhacophoridae, this group of Madagascan frogs are now grouped as a separate family. The genus *Mantella*, after which the family is named, are similar to poison dart frogs in being active by day, brightly coloured, and in the case of some species, toxic.

Family: Microhylidae
Common name: Narrow-mouthed frog
Distribution: North America, South America, southern Africa, and Southeast Asia
Size: 433 species
Description: A widespread group of frogs that have a range of lifestyles. Some are burrowers while others live in trees. All of them have short front legs and a small, pointed mouth.

Family: Myobatrachidae
Common name: Australian water frogs
Distribution: Australia and New Guinea
Size: 126 species
Description: A diverse family of frogs, some of which live in mountain streams; others live buried in dry habitats.

Family: Nasikabatrachidae
Common name: None
Distribution: Western Ghat Mountains in southern India
Size: 1 species
Description: A large burrowing frog with a short head.

Family: Ranidae
Common name: True frogs
Distribution: North America, northern South America, Africa, Europe, and Asia
Size: 822 species
Description: A widespread group that includes true frogs, such as the water frogs, the common frog, the wood frog, and bullfrogs. They have smooth skin and powerful hind legs. The family also contains the largest living species: the Goliath frog (*Conraua goliath*) of West Africa grows to more than 30 cm long.

Family: Rhacophoridae
Common name: African and Asian tree frogs
Distribution: Southern, East, and Southeast Asia, Madagascar, and Sub-Saharan Africa
Size: 293 species
Description: A wide-ranging group of tree frogs, which include the so-called flying frogs. Many lay eggs in foam nests.

Family: Rhinodermatidae
Common name: Mouth-brooding frogs
Distribution: Chile
Size: 2 species
Description: As their name suggests, these frogs have a unique method of caring for their young. The male collects the tadpoles in his vocal sac. In one of the species he then delivers them to a pool of water; in the

other the male broods the young in the mouth for several weeks until they develop into froglets.

Family: Sooglossidae
Common name: Seychelles frogs
Distribution: Seychelles Islands
Size: 4 species
Description: These species have an unusual life cycle. Tadpoles hatch from the egg already with small forelimbs. They use them to crawl onto their mother's back, where they stay until after becoming froglets. The tadpoles do not live in water and so do not have gills (or lungs). Instead they breathe only through the skin.

Order: Caudata (salamanders and newts)

This order, also called Urodela, is divided into three superfamilies: Salamandroidae, Cryptobranchoidea, and Sirenoidea. Key characteristics are a long tail and four small limbs of roughly equal size. The largest subgroup is the Salamandroidae, which contains 90 per cent of species. Its members differ from those of the other two superfamilies in that they reproduce using internal fertilization.

Superfamily: Sirenoidea

Family: Sirenidae
Common name: Sirens
Distribution: Southern United States
Size: 4 species
Description: Eel-shaped aquatic animals that live in muddy water. They prey on crayfish, worms, and snails. The greater siren grows to nearly 1 metre long.

Superfamily: Cryptobranchoidea

Family: Cryptobranchidae
Common name: Giant salamanders and hellbender
Distribution: Eastern United States, Japan, China
Size: 3 species
Description: The largest amphibians of all, ranging from 70 cm to 1.5 metres long. They live underwater but lack gills, breathing through the skin instead. They can only survive in clean, fast-flowing water, with a lot of dissolved oxygen.

Family: Hynobiidae
Common name: Asiatic salamanders
Distribution: Siberia
Size: 52 species
Description: Thought to contain the most primitive amphibians, this family lives underwater in fast-flowing streams. Most lack lungs and several have sharp claws.

Superfamily: Salamandroidea

Family: Ambystomatidae
Common name: Mole salamanders
Distribution: North America
Size: 30 species
Description: This group of salamanders live in burrows as adults., but spend their larval stage in water. During the spring breeding season, these salamanders are seen migrating to pools.

Family: Amphiumidae
Common name: Amphiumas or Congo eels
Distribution: Southern United States
Size: 3 species
Description: Neither eels, nor from the Congo, these snake-shaped amphibians live in swamps in the southern United States. They have a pair of tiny front legs only. They breathe with lungs and might slither onto land after rains. At other times these long (90 cm) amphibians hunt for frogs, fish, and crayfish in water.

Family: Dicamptodontidae
Common name: Pacific giant salamanders
Distribution: Pacific coast of North America
Size: 4 species
Description: Four terrestrial species from the Pacific Northwest whose larva live in fast-flowing mountain streams. They return to streams to breed, and at 35 cm long they are the world's largest terrestrial salamanders.

Family: Plethodontidae
Common name: Lungless salamanders
Distribution: North and South America
Size: 383 species
Description: The largest group of salamanders. Despite having no lungs they are the most terrestrial of amphibians. They breathe through the skin, which must be kept moist. Many species are completely independent of water and lay eggs that hatch into miniature adults.

Family: Proteidae
Common name: Mudpuppies and waterdogs
Distribution: Eastern North America
Size: 6 species
Description: Aquatic amphibians with long bodies, tiny legs, and external gills, even as adults.

Family: Rhyacotritonidae
Common name: Torrent salamanders
Distribution: Pacific coast of North America
Size: 4 species
Description: Sturdy salamanders that live in cold mountain streams. The cold water slows the development of larvae, which take up to five years to reach adulthood. In the coldest parts of their range, some torrent salamanders never take the adult form, but grow sexual organs while still looking and living like larvae.

Family: Salamandridae
Common name: Newts and salamanders
Distribution: North America, Europe, and Southeast Asia
Size: 74 species

Description: The widest-ranging group of salamanders. Most spend most of their lives on land, returning to water to breed. This family includes the fire salamander.

Order: Gymnophonia (caecilians)

These worm-like creatures are thought to have followed a separate evolutionary branch from the rest of the amphibians early in the evolution of the class.

Family: Caeciliidae
Common name: Tailless caecilians
Distribution: Central and South America, East and West Africa, the Seychelles, India and Sri Lanka, Southeast Asia from Bengal to the southern Philippines, and southern China through the Malay Peninsula
Size: 101 species
Description: Live in leaf litter and streams and dig through soil. They sit and wait for worms, insects, and other small prey.

Family: Ichthyophiidae
Common name: Asiatic tailed caecilians
Distribution: India, Sri Lanka, and Southeast Asia
Size: 40 species
Description: Burrowing species that eat mainly worms.

Family: Rhinatrematidae
Common name: American tailed caecilians
Distribution: Northern South America
Size: 9 species
Description: Burrowing species that eat insects and worms.

Family: Scolecomorphidae
Common name: African caecilians
Distribution: Central Africa
Size: 6 species
Description: Burrowing amphibians with tentacles poking out above the eyes. The function of these appendages is unknown.

Family: Typhlonectidae
Common name: Rubber eels
Distribution: South America
Size: 13 species
Description: Aquatic animals that do not lay eggs but give birth to their young. Adults breathe with lungs, while the larvae use gills.

Family: Uraeotyphlidae
Common name: Indian caecilians
Distribution: Southern Asia
Size: 6 species
Description: Small burrowing species that grow to about 25 cm long.

index

278

DK would like to thank:
Steve Willis for his skilful job on the colour
reproduction, and Tim Halliday for advice
on content.

Thomas Marent would like to thank the following
people for their help, support and encouragement:
Carlos Andrés Galvis, Andrés Quintero, Moritz
Grubenmann, Samuel Furrer, Harald Cigler; the
creative team at DK London, especially Helen McTeer,
Tom Jackson, and Ina Stradins.

The publisher would like to thank the following
for their kind permission to reproduce their
photographs:

(Key: a-above; b-below/bottom; c-centre; l-left;
r-right; t-top)

Alamy Images: Arco Images 156b; Ardea: Elizabeth
Bomford 252–53; Corbis: Visuals Unlimited 157;
FLPA: Albert Visage 156t; Mattias Ekstedt
(Sweden): 211; NHPA / Photoshot: Stephen Dalton
170–71; Photolibrary: Berndt Fischer / Oxford
Scientific (OSF) 164–65